The Whisper

Plus

A Guide To Living Free:

28 practical steps to overcoming
sexual abuse

Shirley Jo Petersen

Cedar Hill Publishing

The Whisper – some secrets shouldn't be kept

Cover design by Rebecca Hayes

Cover photo by Nathan Blossom

Book design by Rebecca Hayes

Editing by Amanda Hafner

Published in the United States by
Cedar Hill Publishing
Snowflake, Arizona 85937

ISBN 1-933324-11-2

Library of Congress Control Number 2005926643

For correspondence, books and CD's orders, visit
www.thewhisper.org or email
whisperyoursecret@hotmail.com

The Whisper

He grabbed me and whispered gruffly in my ear
"Never tell anyone for you'd be marked
damaged goods forever.
Besides, no one would ever believe you."

~~~~

An unforgettable journey of how a minister's daughter
transformed her life of shame into a shining light, and
became a champion for incest victims.

Dedicated to

A marvelous man
One who gave me his love as well as his last name.
The one who shares my heartaches as well as my greatest joys.
The person who restored my dignity, and gave me my wings.
The one who demonstrated what God's love is all about.
Someone I wish you knew as well as I do
For then you would be
Extremely blessed
As I am.

My husband

James Clifford Wayne Petersen

Endorsements

This book is not one to be ignored. The topic is one that we would rather have "whispered" but it needs to be shouted. No family however prominent or "Christian" is immune from this problem. As an educator I would encourage every teacher, counselor and administrator to read this book very carefully because there are students just like Shirley who seek refuge in your school, in your classroom-which may be their only safe place. Shirley's experience can enlighten us as to the signs of abuse and it can offer hope to the victims of abuse.

It is a book about abuse but more significantly it is about how one individual survived and then prevailed.

Janice Whelan, Educator

This is a breath of fresh air for any sexual abuse victim. It lightens the burden of guilt that victims feel. You have offered a lifeline to survivors and your credibility as a victim yourself is a powerful motivational factor. You have successfully shown your readers how to turn any tragedy around and make something positive out of a negative happening.

Linda Gregg, RNC
Women's Health Nurse Practitioner

I think one of the remarkable features in your story, and thus your book, is what you tell your readers about your husband, Jim. I have never read a book which has the same potential as this one to guide a survivor to what they can and should do to facilitate healing. Your book will have great appeal to those who need to see the possibilities for healing, but also the possibilities for restoration to an intimate relationship with spouse, children, and family members. Thank you for the privilege of reading your manuscript.

Beth Swagman, BS.
Christian Reformed Church Abuse Prevention Director

I have just finished reading your book and I wanted to thank you for sharing with others your journey to healing after your abuse. I found your book really helpful and encouraging, and it has led me to go on to find help so that I to can find a life worth living after a life time of abuse. Some of my abuse took place in a Christian church where I had gone to try to get away from my abusing father, so I related to how your abuse affected your spirituality and relationship with Jesus. I also play your CD "Whispers From Heaven" and it is beautiful and so peaceful.

Thank You!

Kendra Whitley   United Kingdom

You have given valuable and powerful insight through these pages for anyone wishing to understand and be helped through such victimization as incest. It is an important contribution as well for anyone seeking to recover from other deep and confusing hurts that overwhelm the human spirit. Your story gives such understandable and hopeful lessons for recovery and health for those who search for true fulfillment for their life. It is such a wonderful resource book filled with lessons from Divine Inspiration and important links to other related writings.

Few books grip me but this one tugged at my heart. It inspired and encouraged me personally. Thank you for sharing your story with me.

Walter L. Stump, PhD. Clinical Psychologist

Oh what a terrible, wonderful story. Shirley, you described well the plight of too many girls and articulated well what the journey to recovery looks like. I am so proud of the way you did not let your parents off the hook, yet you extended grace to them. It is true that people with unattended wounds, wound others. You are bringing healing.

Sandy Burdick
Director of Open Hearts Ministry,
author of Secrets of The Heart

This book is a work of grace, God's grace. Because stories of incest leave most of us with unpleasant, confusing, and even overwhelming feelings, we tend to avert our eyes and close our ears to the cries for help of those victimized. Shirley's frank, well told story leads us through and beyond the pain. It tells a journey and healing that point to resources, which were a lifeline for Shirley. I salute Shirley and her family for the courage to share this story with us. May the healing and hope continue as others are guided as they read The Whisper.

Richard A. Westmaas, PhD. Clinical Psychologist

This is a precious document from the heart of a precious person. I believe your testimony is a unique one among all the books and memoirs on the topic of sexual abuse.

Lojan E. LaRowe, PhD. Clinical Psychologist

The Whisper is a heroic story and so innocently direct. I was particularly struck by the pivotal role in the husband, knowing to take the needed measurers to assist in his wife's recovery.

Clark E. Barshinger, PhD Clinical Psychologist
Lajan LaRowe and Clark Barshinger
co-authors of The Haunted Marriage.

This is excellent, excellent material. And you are a gifted storyteller. I admire you so much and I think your book will touch many people. Thank you for sharing your wonderful, important book with me.

Martha Irvine, BA, MA, Journalist

In all the material I have read, I've never come across anything that has given me as much hope and assistance as this one has. I connected with you, and cried with you. You truly have walked in my shoes. Thank you, for sharing your amazing story.

Ellie K. Incest victim

I loved your book. I finally found a book that addresses the seriousness of incest and identifies issues we victims face daily. It is real, and powerful, and most of all it has given me hope and direction.

Lori. G. Incest victim

This chronicle of emotional pain and recovery takes the reader on a journey that touches the heart and soul and no one will be the same after reading this amazing account of abuse and survival.

D. Joyce Kelley, Book editor

Your journey from a victim to an over comer is an inspiration. This is certain to give hope to others seeking a way through a difficult past. Shirley you are a wounded healer and I am certain God will use your story to bless many who need to be renewed.

Rev. Dale Ostema,
Minister of Cadillac United Methodist Church

Shirley pulls no punches telling how she, the victim hid for years the facts from the ones closest to her. She tells how she faced the dreaded revelation and how she overcame her suffering with the help of her husband, family and faith in God. Shirley narrates her personal story so that all of us can understand the struggle and healing in her life. Today we know Shirley as the positive and happy person of her present day and that is inspiration for us all.

Dr. James Wilson,
Medical Director District #10, Cadillac, Michigan

I commend you for trusting God and sharing your most inner self through your book. We are all so afraid to unmask ourselves for fear of being rejected. Your book is such a testimony to God's promise that he will never abandon us, and we need not fear being alone -- ever! With all my heart, I feel your book will allow so many people to face their fears. It truly is a comfort to everyone to know they are not alone. Your book assures everyone who reads it, that regardless of what fear they face, God's promised abundant life awaits them. I have been practicing law for almost 20 years now, and have witnessed people's fears from that perspective. People are so afraid of the truth. I regularly refer your book as a testimony for what wonderful things can happen when the truth is unveiled.

May God bless you and your family.

Kay Grimes, *Attorney at Law, San Antonio Texas.*

Acknowledgements

When I have read books, I've often skipped over the pages that gave thanks and acknowledgements to those who have helped authors with their books. Never again will I do that. I have learned in the process of writing this book that those special people are extremely important agents that God puts in our midst to assist us, and without them these books would never get published, so I applaud you all.

Writing a book is a tedious and consuming project, especially one of this nature, and without the encouragement and inspiration of those *special people* I doubt this book would have ever made the shelf. You were part of God's plan to make this happen and you deserve much more credit than I can give you.

So to you dear friends who have encouraged and prodded me, I give you my heartfelt gratitude. It was your insistence and assistance that made this become a reality.

Linda D. and to Linda G. thanks for your powerful words, "You've got to put your story in a book!"

Joyce K. for giving me my first thesaurus and telling me to get started.

Janice W. for saying, "Great Shirley! I'll be glad to help you". And she did again and again.

Cynthia B. for your gift of time, and willingness to edit each new draft.

Tim O. for your constructive advice and loaning me Stephen King's book *On Writing.*

Martha I., and J. Seward for your amazing words of encouragement.

Rich W., Walter S., Joan I., Ray and Betty M., Donna and Pat M. for your research and assistance in helping me to get this published.

Joan W. for your positive example and for saying "Your story is so amazing, I'm sending your first copy to Oprah!"

Shannon and Paula, who graciously struggled to help me with my first attempts.

To my beloved brothers and sisters, for your tolerance and refreshing my memory.

My dear daughters for your understanding of "why" and loving care through this process.

Jim, my cherished husband,

Your depth of love was shown once again, and your patience was beyond the call of duty. I'm so lucky.

To My Heavenly Father, you gave me the stamina to make it happen, and in the process, changed my life. I am forever grateful.

Shirley Jo Petersen

Special Mention

I'd also like to acknowledge Dr. Robert Schuller. Through the years, he has become an important mentor and made a big impact on my life. His remarkable ability to relate truths cornered my attention. His words planted seeds of hope and encouraged me to dream big, and make something positive out of my unfortunate childhood. Through his ministry I learned it was possible to turn a life of shame into a shining light - giving hope to others.

With gratitude, I thank you.

Definitions:

Sexual abuse is any inappropriate sexual conduct; either verbal, visual or physical that is forced or coerced onto another individual for the reason to sexually stimulate the abuser or, designed to sexually stimulate or harass a victim.

Incest is sexual abuse of a child under the age of 18 by a person who is a member of the child's family or has some type of kinship role in a child's life.

Sexual Abuse Statistics (usgov.statictics.com)

- A rape is reported in the U.S. very three minutes.
- One in three females and one in six males become a victim of sexual abuse before the age of eighteen.
- One in five children is solicited for sex on the internet.
- The most common age for sexual abuse to occur is 6 to 11 years old.
- There are 39 million survivors of childhood sexual abuse in the U.S.
- 49% of the parents blame their child for being sexually abused.
- 90% of Runaways will experience sexual abuse.
- 95% of Prostitutes were sexually abused as children.
- The average age when a victim begins seeking help is 40 years old.

Table of Contents

Prologue

Hurriedly, I pushed through the beauty salon's heavy glass door. The clock on the lavender wall read 5:45 p.m. Shoot, I was late again. I promised myself that wouldn't happen but... it did. An hour earlier, I had stopped at the grocery store to pick up a few items. However, the shortest checkout lane ended up being the slowest line, which made me late once again. Somehow delays are a frequent part of my life in spite of my best efforts.

My hair appointment was the last one of the day. I hoped I could still get it cut and my eyebrows waxed before the busy weekend began.

As I looked past the display of beauty supplies I saw Kurt's pleasant smile. He motioned for me to come on through. I apologized for my tardiness as I hustled toward him.

"So what are you doing these days, and how is your book coming?" asked Kurt as he wrapped the plastic apron around my neck. He lowered the back of the chair down to the sink and began to wash my hair.

"Well," I said, "I finished my book and I'm now in the process of getting it published."

He replied, "Good, that's good. I know your story will help a lot of people."

Listening in on our conversation was an elderly lady sitting immediately to our right. Her silver locks were wrapped in tiny curling rods, waiting for her perm to set.

After the cream rinse, Kurt towel dried my hair and began to comb through the snarls when the little lady asked, "You've written a book?"

I nodded yes.

"I've never known anyone who's written a book. What's it about?" she questioned.

I smiled and replied, "It's a combination autobiography and self-help book. During my childhood I was a victim of incest by my father, who at that time was an influential Protestant minister. At seventeen, I finally found a way to stop the incest. I was so wounded and shamed by that experience that I locked my secret inside for over thirty years. By then, I had anguished so much about my sexual abuse that it had to tumble out.

My book tells about my life as a victim of sexual abuse, and how I eventually found healing." I paused briefly. "I had huge obstacles to overcome, but my health and faith have been restored, and I consider that somewhat of a miracle. I wanted to encourage other victims that wounds of this nature can heal and life can be good, even after incest, so I began writing my story."

Leah, the little lady, began to shake her head and grieve. For a moment all you could hear was the background music coming from the radio. Then she said, "You know, I was a victim of incest, too. I was. It happened over fifty years ago only I've never told anyone about it. I can't believe I just told you. Isn't it funny? I'm telling a stranger my worst secret." She paused for a moment and then added, "Incest is terrible, and it affects your whole life, but no one really knows how bad it is unless they've experienced it, too."

I agreed wholeheartedly with her and told her I was glad she told me. As soon as I finished speaking, she began to tell about her sexual abuse.

Leah was raped in her twenties while still a virgin. Her brother-in-law, a physician, was the perpetrator. This devastated Leah and threw her life into a whirlwind. She ran away from home to escape the memory of her sexual abuse, and started doing things she never dreamed of doing before. She tried everything to cover up her emotional wounds. The rape shattered her life. A while later, she found herself pregnant and single. Leah had her baby and then, for financial reasons, moved back home with her parents. She eventually found a job to support herself and her son. She never married, and devoted the rest of her life to her child. Her parents died never knowing why their beloved daughter turned from her once virtuous ways and became so wild. And what happened to her brother-in-law, the rapist? He died a respected physician. Yep. Life isn't fair.

By now, Kurt had finished trimming my hair and was about to begin the waxing. I reached out to caress Leah's hands as I commended her on her courage for telling her story. I reinforced the importance of her sharing it. Telling is freeing. Leah had just taken an important step. She must have felt tremendously relieved. I know I did for her. For a half a century, Leah had kept her tragedy a secret, and as I listened, I was reminded once again how devastating and shameful incest is. I reminded her she was victimized, an innocent young woman caught in a terrible situation, and what happened to her did not change one ounce of her worth. The shame she embodied belonged to her brother-in-law. She is an incredible lady, and I was thankful I had the chance to meet her and learn about her experience. We agreed to meet again.

More people than we realize are victims of incest and sexual abuse. My counselor told me that one in four females and one in six males are victims of sexual abuse. And because it is such a shameful, degrading experience, most of us hold it in and try to bury the tragedy. For three decades, I kept my abuse hidden. In fact, I was never going to tell anyone. I had planned on taking that secret with me to the grave, but my plan began to crumble as my health and personal life deteriorated. There was no other way to get healthy but to find the courage and start talking about the incest, and so my journey to health began.

In the following pages, I have opened my heart and shared my most intimate experiences. At times the writing was grueling, but I wanted my readers to understand what a troubling life and unbearable shame a victim of incest endures, and also, to what lengths one will go to escape such a life. I hope my honesty will open the eyes of many, and encourage other incest victims to come forth and tell their worst secret. For when they do, it will be the beginning of the end of their true-life nightmare, for telling is transforming.

Writing this autobiography was a difficult task for many reasons. First of all, attempting to write about events that happened over 40 years ago stretched my memory. That is why I found it necessary to pray for wisdom, and consult with family members and friends about many incidents. I am sure this book is not perfect, but I have tried to do my best to make it as truthful as possible.

When incest has occurred in the home, you can be sure that other forms of abuse occurred as well. In addition to sexual abuse, I experience emotional abuse, verbal abuse, physical abuse, spiritual abuse and abandonment issues. I did not realize the depth of my abuse until I began my journey to freedom. Because of my dysfunctional childhood home, I found I needed to make a lot of changes as I faced the depth of my own dysfunctions.

There are life long, crippling consequences that piggyback incest and sexual abuse. Until we tell our stories and expose how horrible it is, and those who do it, we won't have a chance at eliminating sexual abuse from our society. Nor will there be opportunities for us to find healing. I am convinced that as my voice is heard others will dare to share their experiences as well. This is already beginning to happen. Others, like Leah, have come forth and told me their story.

If you were raised in a Judeo-Christian home, you will easily understand the added frustrations I encountered.

Because my abuser was also a minister, my faith was greatly compromised, and at times nullified, by what went on in my household. Consequently, I struggled with many issues. Most understandable was the sexual abuse and the intense hatred I had for my father. Second was my disillusionment with the Christian faith and the God my father professed to know.

For a time, I considered my father and religion useless. On my journey to find peace and wholeness, I eventually learned to dissolve my hatred. I was also able to reclaim my faith in God, which I consider somewhat of a miracle.

Hope was another important attribute that helped me get through my roughest time. If you come away with anything after reading my story, I hope I have given you hope, for you too can break from your past and the baggage that comes with it. I can personally testify that miracles of the heart do happen, and it's my prayer that all victims will experience the same wonder.

We victims of sexual abuse do not realize how badly crippled we really are. We try our best to function normally. To us, it seems like we are doing pretty well in spite of our abuse. The truth is, we think we are doing better than we really are. Only when we take a good look at the seriousness of our abuse, our childhood environment, and evaluate ourselves relationally, will we see how much our sexual abuse has negatively impacted our lives.

As you read my story and journey with me, you will realize that this is hardly a joy ride. Yet, the personal benefits I received at the end certainly made it a remarkable ride. The peace and health I gained are like none I had ever known, and as an added bonus, I was able to experience and return a love that I never knew existed. I only wish I had started my journey much sooner. I can never retrieve those lost years, but if I could, it would have eliminated much heartache in the years that followed the incest.

I have included an important second part to this book. It is a guide to living free from sexual abuse, which includes 28 steps that helped free me from the consequences of the incest. There are actual things we can do to stop a horrendous past from ruining our lives. The purpose of this segment is to empower victims to begin their own personal journey, and experience peace and wholeness.

During our lifetimes, we each struggle with a secret pain, a private unexposed wound. Sexual abuse, abandonment issues, alcoholism, and relationship problems are a few examples. How we handle those hurts will greatly affect the quality of our lives. The lessons I've learned on my journey to wholeness were lifesaving to me. I believe the same principles will also add insight to those who suffer with similar issues that crush the spirit. And if you are a victim of sexual abuse, please continue reading for The Whisper was especially written for you. There may be parts that are difficult to read, but ***don't stop reading.*** There are many mini messages throughout the book that will help you on your healing journey.

Passing Hope On ~

Shirley Jo Petersen

To You My Friend

If I could take your pain away
And make today like yesterday
I would for you, My Friend

If I had the power to turn the tide
To move the hands and change the time
Back to before it all began
Yes, that's what I would do

Oh, Dear Friend
My heart weeps a sad refrain
Let me help absorb your pain
And if there is any solace
In knowing your sorrow is shared
A prayer is answered

You are not alone, Dear One
We share a kinship of the heart
For I too know the pangs of woe
I've worn the mask of shame
Come—take my hand
Dance with me in the Holy Light
That melts away the pain.

1

If only there was a simple delete key for the pain in the human heart.

It was one of those perfect, warm summer evenings in July of 1991. Not too hot or humid, a perfect night for great sleeping. My husband Jim and I were lying comfortably in our queen size bed, enjoying the quiet breeze that flowed gently through our upstairs bedroom window. Even Lake Cadillac, which lay only 50 feet in front of our bedroom, seemed especially calm as the bright moonlight reflected its loveliness. There was a special serenity about that particular evening. Maybe it was just the delightful night, or because the house was especially quiet, or because I was anticipating the wonderful week ahead of being "childless." However, what made it exceptional is what transpired during the course of that evening. Those events marked the beginning of my liberation from a past that had brought me much pain and shame.

Earlier that day, Jim and I had taken our girls to camp and I was looking forward to a time of respite from being the busy mother of three. I had plans for reading a few books and wallpapering the downstairs bathroom. My mind was busy with anticipation of all I would get done, when I felt Jim ease his way over toward my side of the bed. His hand reached for my thigh and then continued to slide upwards underneath my nightgown. It was obvious that he had different plans for the time we would have alone.

As I felt his touch, I quickly rolled on my left side away from him as I had so many times before, and thought, "Oh, how I wish I could enjoy my husband and all the love he wanted to give me." But I couldn't. I couldn't even pretend to enjoy it anymore. Jim's touch triggered repulsive memories of my youth when I had to tolerate the gross, unwanted touches of my father. The less I let Jim touch me, the less the haunting memories would plague me.

Who would have thought that Jim's soft hands and loving gestures would set my mind in such a spin, to make me relive all the times my father had sexually abused me? Certainly not me, but they did. And the sad thing is, Jim had no idea why I responded so coolly to him. My actions greatly concerned him, and brought him heartache and frustration. The terrible shame I harbored kept me from telling him or anyone else about the incest. Also, my father's words, "You are a used rag and no one would want you if they knew," left a deep imprint. My sexual abuse was one secret I had planned on taking with me to my grave. The humiliation from that experience was so severe that I never wanted to relive it again. However, now thirty years later, I began to realize that something had to give pretty soon, for the cruel affects from the incest were spilling into every area of my life. It was not only interfering with my marriage, my health, and relationships, but also affecting the parenting of my children.

While I was lying on my side of the bed that evening, Jim removed his hand and then lovingly put his arm over my waist as he cuddled into me. I quietly breathed a sigh of relief. I loved and craved his gestures of tenderness, but so disliked my reactions to our sexual intimacy that I avoided it as much as I could.

Jim's patience that evening was evident once again. He was such a wonderful husband and deserved much more than I could give him. The remorse I felt for having such an ugly secret—and for keeping it from him—was nearly killing me. I was so overwhelmed with grief that I began to weep.

"Why are you crying, Shirl? Is it something I did?" Jim's caring words that evening began the dreaded, yet long needed, conversation.

I replied, "No, it's not you, and it never has been you."

"Well, what is it? Is it another man?" was his insightful response.

I managed to nod my head yes, then I said, "I have something terrible to tell you. I should have told you this a very long time ago, but I was too ashamed." Jim listened intently. "It's something my father did to me while I was growing up." Then I began to sob so hard, I couldn't continue.

Jim surmised what had happened and said, "Did your father sexually abuse you?" I nodded my head yes, and quivered with shame as I pulled the comforter up over my head. He embraced me ever so lovingly, and then became silent. I lay in that fetal position weeping, with Jim's arms around me for a few moments until I noticed an eerie stillness. I thought to myself, *What is Jim thinking? Does he still want me? Is he mad at me? Is he going to go kill my father? Could he still love me now that he knows what happened to me?*

In the quiet night, my father's words echoed loudly in my head. "Don't ever tell anyone because no one would want you if they knew. No one wants damaged goods." Even though Jim had proven his love for me time and again, I was still petrified by what his response might be.

Jim remained quiet. He was stunned by the news and didn't know what to say or think first. Finally, he said, "Shirley, you don't have any idea how much I love you and have loved you all these years, do you? If you had, you would have told me this from the beginning. I love you so much." After a moment's pause, he continued, "I can't believe you held this from me for the past twenty-five years. This is mind-boggling. I don't know what to say. I thought we had been truthful about everything and now I can't help but wonder if our life is filled with other secrets I should know about." Then more tears began to flow.

In the hours that followed, Jim's questions poured on. As I answered, flashbacks of the abuse became as vivid as if the incest had occurred only yesterday. I found it amazing how quickly my mind recalled the sounds and smells I had experienced so many years ago. It was as if the dark cloud I experienced as a teenager had reappeared. Along with the shocking, sordid details came years of bottled up emotions. My tears flowed as if they were washing my heart clean of every bit of shame and filth I had harbored from the very beginning of the sexual abuse. When a child, I was rebuked for crying and learned to choke down my emotions and swallow my tears. But now, in Jim's arms, it was safe to cry and *wow*, what a healthy cleansing that was.

Jim wept with me as he expressed his sorrow for what had happened many years ago. He also shared his remorse for not picking up on the sexual abuse, for the signs were all there. However, because my father was a minister, incest had never entered his mind. Jim's anger and disgust for my father grew by the moment.

As our sleepless night slowly crept into a new dawn, Jim and I became aware that we were not only beginning a new day, but also starting a new chapter in our marriage. The journey on which we were about to embark would bring about many changes and ultimately enhance our relationship more than we could imagine.

That night, my husband intervened and became my true hero. Jim's powerful aura of love penetrated my wounded heart. It was awesome, as if he absorbed my pain and shame, for I no longer felt the heavy burden I had carried around for all those years. My burden quickly became his, and he gallantly rose to the occasion to become my advocate and protector. For the very first time in my life, I was not alone with my problem. Finally, someone had come to rescue me, or, I should say, finally I *allowed* someone to rescue me, and through Jim, I experienced a love I never knew existed.

Exposing my story was excruciating. The shame was so intense it left me emotionally paralyzed. For a while, I didn't have the wits to think or speak for myself. Jim instinctively picked up on my needs and took over. Even now, when I look at Jim, I get an overwhelming sense of gratitude for all he has done for me.

As you might have surmised, the tears and grieving process lasted more than just one evening. In fact, it took many months, for the sorrow was plenty, and the hurt very deep.

As we talked through the night, Jim's eyes kept darting toward the phone on our nightstand. He was anxiously waiting to confront my father. At 7:00 a.m., he picked up the phone and within seconds was talking to him. Jim's fury demanded a meeting immediately face to face with both my parents in our home. I could never imagine such a meeting by myself. My childhood fears prohibited it, but with Jim taking control, I believed I would survive the ordeal.

Confronting my abuser was important for my healing, even if it was extremely difficult. I was amazed at Jim's tenacity and courage to make it happen.

I heard author and inspirational speaker Paula White say that you can't conquer what you won't confront. That small statement packs a big truth.

I had doubts that my father would admit to the incest. I knew the truth, but I doubted he would ever come clean. If anything, I hoped that expressing my emotional pain to the one who caused it would bring some peace of mind. Besides, Jim was right. It was time for my father to be made accountable and pay the consequences for his sick sins.

I think my father knew that dreaded phone call would come one day. He had gotten away with a very serious crime for many years. You might say that it was his *moment of truth,* and he had a lot of explaining to do.

My husband's call forced my father to do some quick talking, not only to Jim, but also to my mother who, at that time, claimed she knew nothing of the incest. We learned later, during a counseling session, that she had blocked out most of her memory during those twelve dark years. It was her way of coping with troubles she didn't know how to handle.

The day after Jim's call, my parents drove the 250 miles north to see us. I watched through our kitchen window as they got out of their car and sheepishly walked up the sidewalk to our house. I called for Jim. Immediately, he came to the door to let them in. My stomach ached, and my legs shook. I was literally sick from the whole ugly situation. Then I glanced at Jim. He stood straight and tall, eager to confront my abuser. Jim's strong sense of what is right and wrong made this task a relatively easy one for him. However, when he first saw my father, it took all the strength he had not to lay him flat. He was beyond furious with both my parents. He ushered them into the family room and ordered them to sit down. I followed like a frightened mute.

"All right, Dad, I want to know exactly what you did do to Shirley," Jim's interrogation began. "Shirley has told me everything, so you better be truthful and don't hold anything back."

I sat motionless, rigid as a rock, as I listened to my father shamefully tell how the sexual abuse had happened. Jim's eyes glanced at me and then kindly said, " Shirl, would you and your mother go up to the living room so I can talk to your father alone?" He sensed how painful this was for me and wanted to spare me from any further agony. My mother and I gladly complied.

In the living room, my mother began to voice words of remorse. While staring at the carpeted floor she said, "Honey, I had no idea this ever happened. I can hardly believe it did. I feel so terrible about it." She paused, still staring at the floor.

Disheartened by her comment, I responded, "How could that be, Mother? Don't you remember seeing father in bed with me when you were saying bedtime prayers with the twins in their bed, right across from mine?"

"Yes," she began to nod. "But I didn't suspect anything. I was just glad he was showing some interest in at least one of the children."

"Didn't you think it was a little unusual, Mom, that he was laying on me, and kissing and hugging me like I was his wife? And what did you think he was doing there anyway?" I asked.

"Oh, cuddling, I guess," was her weak reply.

"Mom, he was getting himself aroused for the coming late-night sexual escapade," I continued. "And Mom, what about all the times I begged you for help, but you refused to do anything?" My mother just shook her head in disbelief.

I felt ashamed for venting on her as strongly as I did, but I wanted her to know exactly what had gone on. She shared her deep remorse; however, she pleaded with me not to go public. The shame was just too great for her to bear. She was also afraid of what the story would do to the Christian boarding school for troubled teens my father had started, and I think, to her reputation as well. As I listened, I realized her first concern was once again for my father rather than for my welfare. Later, when I told Jim about my mother's comments, he was outraged and was convinced more than ever that she was an enabler to my father's crime.

Meanwhile, downstairs, Jim continued to pump questions at my father. He listened to the ugly deeds my father had committed, not only to me but also to others. Through Jim's probing, we learned that my father was a pedophile, for he admitted to having sex with other young girls. He also told Jim things about our incestuous relationship that I had buried. Before the day was through, my father had sufficiently answered all of Jim's questions, at least for the time being. I had nothing more I wanted to say, either. My parents left, fearful and broken.

That afternoon was uncomfortable and sobering for us all. However, it was a relief that my father admitted to the incest. At least he had courage enough to confess his wrongdoings, and that was a big relief. So many times, perpetrators never "fess up", and that adds another dimension of pain. My father had been living with the burden of his sins for a long time. Maybe it was because he was seventy and deep down, he was ready to be relieved of his guilt before the time came for him to meet his "Maker".

After my parents left, Jim and I lay on the couch, embracing each other like a cocoon. We needed time to assimilate, and recover from that ordeal, and I needed time to think about what I wanted to do next. Jim reminded me that it was my decision, and whatever I decided, he was behind me 110%. I decided to move ahead and to get as healthy as I could, even if it meant exposing the story. I wanted my life with Jim and my children to be the best I could make it.

The relief I experienced after my father admitted to the incest was short-lived. Knowing my family and other close friends would soon learn about the incest made this a very anxious time. Depression began to loom like a thick morning fog. I was ashamed beyond words for others to learn what my father had done to me. I had put on, covered up, and lied about my father's behavior my whole life. I was not a loved child like many people assumed, but a used child, a pawn he wanted only for his sexual gratification. To know that truth was one thing, but to have to admit it and say those words out loud was extremely painful, for isn't your father the one who is supposed to protect and love you? I felt the whole world was looking at the blanket of filth that I believed covered me.

I remember walking down the street one fall day in 1991. I was afraid to look anyone in the eye for fear of what the reaction might be. Even when Jim looked at me, I wondered if I repulsed him. That is why I soaked in his healing words when he said, "Shirl, you are an innocent victim here. What your father did to you does not change the way I feel about you in any way, shape, or form. It only makes me want to love you more. It was a horrible, despicable thing your father did, but you're a wonderful, loving person. That's why I married you. I love you no less because of what your father did to you. The only thing I am disappointed in is that you didn't tell me this much earlier." His soothing words began the shedding of my thick layer of shame.

For months after the "truth bomb" hit, Jim would repeatedly ask, " Shirl, is there anything else you haven't told me?" When I would say, "no," he would reply, "are you sure? You know, don't you, that you can tell me anything?" He had prepared himself for the worst scenario possible and wanted to let me know I could tell him anything, no matter how shocking it might be. I was so thankful there wasn't any more to tell, for what I had already shared was huge enough.

Jim and I told our three daughters about my sexual abuse shortly after I told Jim. It wasn't pleasant telling them about their grandfathers' evil sins. Joanna, our oldest daughter, was twenty-one and living on her own when she heard the story, and she was outraged. Her immediate response was that my father needed to be behind bars *right then*. She called me nearly every day from her home to offer support, yet at the same time was furious that I had not taken the steps to put him in jail. She would say to me, "I mean it, Mom, he needs to be in jail!" I understood her anger. I had considered that option myself. There needs to be consequences for those who commit such crimes, or they will never stop. The truth of the matter was that I wasn't emotionally strong enough to take him to court. That decision would have to come later. I was too emotionally fragile and depressed, for I was still bearing the shame and humiliation for my father's sinful sexual behaviors. I was having a hard enough time just keeping myself together. For the time being, I wanted to spend my energy taking care of my immediate family and work through the difficulties that Jim and I had. I also wanted time to go through family counseling with my parents and my six siblings without having to do it through a jail cell. Time was also a factor. Because my father had cancer, I didn't know how much longer he would live.

The story broke when our two younger daughters were in their teens: Elizabeth, 15, and Diane, 13. They also hurt for me and were sickened and confused by their grandfather's double standards. Their main concern was for my welfare, and their compassion was demonstrated to me daily. Elizabeth and Diane were both athletes and excellent students, which fortunately kept them very busy. I remember missing Elizabeth's sixteenth birthday while I was involved in family counseling in Ft. Lauderdale, Florida. It was a debilitating time, so much so that I forgot to pick up the phone and call her. Thankfully, she got over that disappointment long before I did. "Debilitating" is an accurate word to describe the depression I found myself in.

Fortunately, I would learn that the gloom I was experiencing would be replaced with wonderful years of self-confidence and peace, but until that happened, I had to trudge through a difficult time. Those days seemed to pass slowly, but that period was an essential time of growth. Later, I realized it was the most enlightening and educational time of my life.

Jim and I spent countless hours talking, though Jim did more listening than talking. He encouraged me to talk about anything and at any time, and I did. I also saw a counselor and began reading all I could on sexual abuse. I spent hours at the piano plunking away, making up new tunes, and somehow the music did wonders for my spirit. I searched for resources that would aid me in my recovery, and almost daily I was consoled and encouraged by someone in my family.

Old wounds were finally getting the attention they needed, and my journey to find health and peace was on its way.

2

Sometimes we have to go back to the beginning to learn to live again.

I don't believe anyone enjoys revealing the dark events in their background, and that certainly includes me. It has taken years for me to be comfortable enough to share my story. So much of it is not pleasant; besides, I never liked depressing stories or those with sad endings, so why would I write about such a time in my life? Truthfully, if my life had not had a happy ending, I would not have bothered.

I thank God my life story *does* have a happy ending in spite of my childhood abuse, and because it does, I dare to revisit those difficult days and relay my experiences to you. More significant than my story is how I overcame the consequences that followed the abuse, and that is why I've included the second part of this book "A Guide To Living Free". I eventually learned how to forgive my father and construct a wonderful new life. And believe me, forgiving my father was the last thing I wanted to do, but I found it was an important ingredient in my healing.

In my youth, I was taught a Christian has to forgive and forget. After what I experienced, I knew both were impossible so I abandoned the idea and through God's requests were outrageous. But later, when I learned the truth about forgiveness and whom it benefits (me), I was able to revisit that possibility and eventually relinquish my hate and unforgiveness. I explain more about that later on. Once I forgave my father and mother I began to see a significant difference in my peace and well being for I had let my hate and unforgiveness go, which gave me more energy to focus on my family and my dreams. Today my haunting memories are gone and I never think of my sexual abuse except when I am asked to speak or share my story.

My earliest recollection of sexual abuse began when I was at the tender age of four. I remember as if it were only yesterday, when my father called me into his upstairs parsonage bedroom in Belvedere, Illinois. What he revealed to me when he pulled down his boxer shorts was a sight I should never have been forced to see. As he pulled me toward him, all I could do was shut my eyes and lunge away. Eventually, he let go of my hand, and I ran down the stairs and out of the house as far and fast as my chubby legs would take me. Ironically, that is exactly how the incest finally ended some thirteen years later. I found myself running down the stairs away from my father and out of the parsonage in Plainwell, Michigan. That time, however, I knew I would never have to go back again...ever.

Before I go any further into my story, I would like to introduce you to family members who played key roles in my life and enlighten you as to how their lives and behaviors contributed to my story. To protect their privacy, their names have been changed.

William and Doris Lillie, my father's parents, were born and raised in the small village of Sparta, Michigan. They began their rocky 54-year relationship in high school in 1919. Doris's parents were well-respected people in their community. Her father was the town mayor, and also the town barber, and knew everyone. When they became aware of their youngest daughter's new boyfriend, William, they discouraged her from seeing him. William's father had the reputation of being a womanizer and a drunk. His family was definitely not part of their inner circle of friends, nor was William an approved young man for her to date. However, strong-willed Doris was determined to carry on a relationship with her new sweetheart, even if it had to be done in secrecy. Their courtship became intimate, and in June 1920, just after they both graduated from high school, my grandmother found herself pregnant with my father. Realizing the terrible embarrassment this would bring to her family, Doris made several attempts to self-abort, but to no avail. Eventually the unpleasant dilemma she found herself in became evident. Doris's parents were devastated, but had no choice but to bear the shame and accept their new son-in-law into the family.

Two months after their marriage, Doris and William's baby boy Martin was born on March 31, 1921. The following September, Doris and William both went off to college in Davenport, Iowa, to become chiropractors. Obviously, their marriage got off to a very difficult start. Unfortunately, it continued to be plagued with more difficulties when my grandfather began patterns of infidelity.

My father had been an unwanted child since his conception and was caught in an unwanted marriage where love ran thin. His parents' resentment only grew as he did. He was battered and emotionally abused, shunned and often forced to eat his meals outside and alone. For seven years, my father was the only child. Then four more boys were born into their family. They each have their own eventful family stories to tell.

For more than fifty years, my grandparents remained married, but seemed locked into their unhappy relationship, for divorce was very much a disgrace in those days. As a child, I remember visiting their large, lovely home. My grandmother cared for me while my mother was having babies, and I witnessed firsthand the strong hostility between her and my grandfather. Their home echoed with unpleasant words and discontent. In spite of its size and beauty, their home, to me, was a daunting place to visit.

When my grandmother was in her sixties, she suffered a severe stroke. I always thought it was from the large amount of stress in her life. A year later, she fell and broke her hip. During the time of her recovery and until her death, my grandfather took care of her, and I saw a redeeming side of him that I carry with me to this day.

My father, raised in that dysfunctional environment, experienced many difficult years growing up. His childhood was split between living at home, staying with his grandparents, and staying at boarding schools. After he was kicked out of Howe Military Academy in Culver, Indiana, his problems continued, and he was often in trouble for breaking the law. From 1935 through 1938, my father was sent to the Starr Commonwealth Home for Boys in Albion, Michigan. For his senior year of high school, he was sent to live with his Uncle Matt and Aunt Millie, his father's brother and sister-in-law, in North Adams. It was not possible for him to return home because of the strained relationship between him and his parents. It was there, in the tiny village of North Adams, Michigan, where the fate of my future began, for that is where my father first met my mother.

My mother's parents lived a more blessed life. While visiting his relatives in Ontario, Canada, Laurence Stone, my mother's father, met a special beauty that conveniently lived next door to his relatives. Louise Lattimore, my mother's mother, had recently returned home from finishing school, where she had learned the art of being a proper wife and how to run a smooth household. Laurence was smitten with her charm and wit, and their romance began. They were married in 1908, after which Laurence moved his new bride to Detroit, Michigan, where he worked as an electrical engineer. From there, the devoted Christian couple moved wherever his work took them. My grandmother was a constant delight and helpmate to my grandfather for more than seventy years as well as a devoted mother to their son and four daughters.

In the early 1930s, our nation was in the throes of the Great Depression. During that time, Grandfather Stone moved his family from Chicago to North Adams, Michigan, where he bought a dairy farm to feed his family and to weather out the Depression. While working as an engineer in Chicago, my grandfather's specialty had been making production lines go more smoothly. Now this novice farmer was challenged to use his expertise on the farm to make it produce enough to feed his large household.

The Stone family considered themselves fortunate to have a home and plenty of food on their table during those difficult years. Eventually, as other family members lost their jobs, aunts, uncles, and cousins moved in with them on the farm. They divided their bedrooms into living quarters so each family would have a space of their own. At mealtime, the women would gather to prepare the food while the men worked on the farm.

Adel, my mother, was nine years old when her family moved from Chicago to North Adams. Even as the youngest of five children, she learned early what hard work was and did her fair share around the farm. Before school, she would peddle milk with her dad. She would sit on the back of a horse drawn cart and sell bottles of milk for 5 cents a quart. After school, there were milk cans to scrub and a multitude of other household chores, which were shared by her four siblings. Those close to her said my mother's sweet disposition and pretty face added a special charm to those difficult times.

It was there, in North Adams, in the summer of 1938, when my father's deep-set blue eyes first glanced at my mother's innocent face. This was just before their senior year of high school. They first became friends through their activities at church. My father's Uncle Matt was the minister of the little Bible church in North Adams, and my father was required to attend all the services as long as he was living with them.

Laurence and Louise Stone were concerned about their daughter's newfound male friend. Martin Lillie already had quite a checkered history, so they discouraged any kind of relationship with him. My mother naturally shied away from him, for she, too, had reservations about him, and besides, she was busy with her many friends and activities. She also had a big schoolgirl's crush on a young man who also attended her church and was planning on becoming a missionary. She had always wanted to be a missionary herself and dreamed of being in that position beside him.

However, my father was deeply infatuated with my mother and wouldn't let up until she agreed to at least an afternoon date, which unfortunately ended up disastrous.

That autumn afternoon, while riding horseback with my mother in a wooded area near her family farm, my father forced himself upon my mother. She became a victim of date rape, which didn't have a name back then. She kept this excruciating event hidden for more than 50 years. It wasn't until I broke with my story in 1991 that my mom shared hers with me. Being a virgin was extremely important to my mother, as it was to many girls in those days. She wanted to save her first sexual experience for her husband. How could she ever tell her husband that she wasn't a virgin? She couldn't. She thought everyone would blame her for allowing it to happen. And they would have back then. Soon the shame became too much, so my mother decided to break off her friendships with both young men without telling a soul the real reason. She decided she would continue her plan to be a missionary, but remain unmarried.

Church activities were highlighted events for the Stone family. They seldom missed the two worship services on Sunday or the mid-week prayer meeting. The same was true for the pastor's family and their live-in guest, my father.

My father relentlessly pursued my mother at church and at school, for he was determined to win her affection. However, she repeatedly refused to have anything to do with him. After graduation, my mother moved to Chicago and began her education to become a missionary by attending Moody Bible Institute. Her oldest sister and husband conveniently lived in Chicago, so she roomed in with them. To help support herself, she worked on the weekends as a nurse's aide at the Cook County Hospital.

That same summer, my father went to barber school in southern Michigan. When fall arrived, he attended Adrian College in Adrian, Michigan. While there, he was very much alone, which provided time to do some serious soul-searching. He realized he had screwed up his life, and he needed God's intervention to help him change his ways. One evening, in his desperation and gloom, he asked God to come into his life and help him. Feeling renewed and hopeful, he wanted to share the good news with my mother, so he drove to Chicago to tell her. He did his best to convince her that he was a changed man and asked her to marry him. My mother was very skeptical, for the rape incident was still very clear and painful. Eventually, she agreed, if he would go to college and become a minister. She thought that would truly make a changed man out of him. Later, my mom told me that she thought she could never marry anyone else except my father because of what he had done to her. In her eyes, if she ever wanted a family and children, it had to be with him. She decided to make the best of their life together and was content to be a minister's wife. Besides, she thought being a minister's wife was sort of like being a missionary. Immediately, my father began making plans to attend a Bible college while my mother made plans for a spring wedding.

World War II was in full force at this time, and my father was required to cut soldiers' hair stateside for six months before he went to Bible College. The following April 6, 1941, my mother became Mrs. Martin Lillie, and the two of them went off to New York State so my father could begin his education to become a minister. My mother eagerly looked upon every church my father ministered as a mission field to serve God.

Reading Center Community Church in New York became the first church my father pastored. New York also became the birthplace of their first three children: David, Naomi, and me. From there, our family moved to various places as my father accepted different church pastorate positions. Belvedere, Illinois, was where my brother Joshua and my twin sisters Georgia and Ginger were born. While ministering there, my father became very ill with pneumonia. His doctor urged him to go to a warmer climate to recover. He took his physician's advice, packed up the family, and jammed our meager belongings into a 28-foot travel trailer, and for six months, we lived in Syracuse, Florida. The warm Gulf climate worked, and my father recovered.

By the spring of 1954, we were back in Michigan. We temporarily parked our gray travel trailer behind my mother's parents' home in Jonesville and camped there until my father found a church to pastor. I remember that short period of time as very pleasant. It was the first I'd experienced connectedness and love from extended family members such as grandparents, aunts, uncles, and cousins.

Education was never a priority for us children. We were pulled out of several different schools as we moved, always during the middle of the school year. This made it difficult to keep up with our grades. While in Florida, we never opened a schoolbook, so we lost ground again. Though challenging, we children managed to get through high school and then went on to further our education with various degrees.

From 1954 to1956, we enjoyed rural living in the tiny town of Tipton, Michigan, while my father ministered at the Community Church. The church folk thought he could walk on water as he packed their small church Sunday after Sunday. My father had a certain amount of charisma and was a Bible scholar, so he knew how to preach an interesting sermon. But it was my mother who was the real saint in making the church succeed, for she ran the Sunday school, youth groups, choirs, and women's fellowship. Many admired her.

In 1956, my father took a three-year break from church work to become Chaplain and Director of Home Life at Starr Commonwealth Home for Boys in Albion, Michigan. He bought an 80-acre farm ten miles north of Albion to park his family on while he attempted to make us into little farmers. At Starr, my father seized the opportunity of having free labor, bringing boys home in the summer and weekends to work the farm. They planted and weeded vegetables. Once my father dropped the boys off and instructed them what to do, he left. My oldest brother David, who was only 14 and 15 at the time, was given the responsibility of being their chore master and was ordered to whip them into shape if necessary. We also had a few goats, sheep, pigs, chickens, and beehives, which received inadequate care, for we were very ignorant about farming.

Having the teenage boys around was not pleasant; in fact, I was scared to death of most of them. A few would try to take advantage of us girls and make remarks that were inappropriate. I remember one pulling me down in the ditch by the cucumber patch and lying on top of me while smashing a hard kiss on my mouth. At twelve, it was very frightening. Others would ask to hold my hand. Most of the boys were just lonely and in desperate need of some TLC, so they volunteered to come to the farm hoping to get some. Besides, it was a change of pace from their boarding school.

Over the years, I watched my petite mother work from morning to night as she unselfishly cared for us. During those three years on the farm, she was isolated from female companionship and the church work she loved so much. She told me it was the unhappiest time in her life. In the summers, she would send my siblings and me to stay with friends or off to camps for weeks at a time. As I look back, I realize it was to alleviate her workload, and just maybe to keep us safe.

While at Starr Commonwealth, my father enjoyed working closely with the founder, Floyd Starr. Floyd had been a positive father figure to him during his teen years when he was a student there. Albion also became the birthplace of our brother Benjamin, the youngest of the seven children. My mother had seven children and one difficult miscarriage in the first fourteen years of marriage, which, needless to say, taxed her strength and spirit.

The years my mother was a pastor's wife were extremely busy ones, and it seemed her work was never done. Many of the Sunday school classes were held at our home, the parsonage, in various rooms including the basement and bedrooms. Every Sunday morning, she would straighten the house and put chairs out before the classes began, all while she prepared a large Sunday dinner. She devotedly attended to her tasks in the church and parsonage, with rarely a complaint. However, because Sundays were so hectic, she usually ended up with a terrible headache at the end of the day. In many respects, she was like a single mom of seven children. And because my father's philosophy was that children and housework were strictly woman's work, he refused to help with any of the domestic work or childcare. I recall one Sunday morning, when my mother asked my father to hold one of the twins. They were ten months old. She was caring for the other twin and needed a helping hand. He reluctantly held one twin briefly out on his knee and gruffly said, "Hurry up, Adel, she's liable to puke on me!" That was the first and last time I ever remember my father holding any of his children.

My mother's pleasant personality had a great influence on her children, and because of her, people thought we were a relatively normal family. In reality, we were far from it.

My mom's motto was "bloom where you are planted". She lived by that rule and made the best of her life wherever her husband led her. She never found fault with anyone, and that included her husband. Her cheerful nature was contagious. Whenever she did see a problem, she gave it up to God in prayer and then ignored it. I maintain she did this to a fault.

ABOVE: Shirley's family in 1951

LEFT: Shirley on the right with her older sister.

RIGHT: Shirley's parents on their wedding day.

LEFT: Shirley with her younger twin sisters.

"Behind The Parsonage Door"

The Church had a parsonage and those within
Were the pastor, his family, and perhaps some kin.
A light in the darkness, one might think it to be
A symbol of help for others to see.

But oh, not so, when you walked through our door
For ours had a stench of shame at its core
Hidden behind the starched shirt, suit, and tie
Lived a life of confusion, sin, and lies.

Forced to act on each demand,
The household jumped at his command.
For to spare the rod was to waste the whip;
Our house of fear was quite a trip.

The worst was yet to come, you see.
My bed, his playpen—oh, how could it be?
Months became years of agonizing grief
Before I escaped and found relief.

The time has come for all to be known
For I am now grown, and no longer alone.
The hidden shame that lurked in my past
Is now history and, thank God, I'm free at last!

SJP

3

Living in a glass house could be a good thing.

The 1960s, when my sexual abuse became the most intense, in many ways mirrored politically much of what we are experiencing today. There was the Russian/Cuban conflict that put many in a panic and, later, the war with Vietnam that fragmented our society. We saw our closest friends and relatives being shipped off to a country we knew little about. The draft was activated, and every young man feared his number would be called. We stored up on food and household products; we cleaned and restocked our fall-out shelters from the '50s; and my father even brought out the gas masks. There were peace marches on campuses across our country. Our nation's problems tripled on the home front with the assassination of President John F. Kennedy, the murder of civil rights leader Rev. Martin Luther King, Jr., and then the killing of Senator and presidential candidate Robert Kennedy. During those turbulent times, we learned that life was fragile as our country mourned our great losses. It was obvious even then that "homeland security" was very weak.

Those were also the days when a loaf of bread cost 25 cents, a gallon of gasoline was 35 cents, a postage stamp 5 cents. You could buy a new Chevy for less than $2,800. Health insurance was not needed, because medical costs were affordable and unemployment was nearly nonexistent. We also received our polio vaccines on a sugar cube instead of by injection.

For me to revisit the '60s brings many uncomfortable memories. Yet, none of them overshadowed the perverted battle I was experiencing as a young teenager in our house in Plainwell, Michigan.

I was thirteen years old when we moved into the parsonage of the church my father was to minister. It was a comfortable, nearly new two-story wooden structure with a lovely sandstone brick front. It was built right next door to the church, a common practice in that era. Our house replaced the previous parsonage that sat immediately to the west. That was a three-story old white Victorian structure, with a large wrap-around porch. Only a narrow dirt driveway divided the two houses. The large Victorian house was the home of our neighbors, Skip and Betty Sanderson, whose eight children and dozens of pets made good use of every corner of the big house. It also became a wonderful house for me, a safe haven to which I would often escape.

Fortunately for me, the Sandersons had five daughters, three of whom were close to my age, and I loved them dearly. Their daughter Sherry and I were cheerleaders together in high school, and we spent countless hours practicing our cheers and jumping on an old inflated tractor inner tube in her back yard. We shared our fantasies and hopes for the future, but I never dared to share what my father was doing to me behind my bedroom door. I relived those wonderful activities with Sherry over and over in my mind. It was the diversion I used to close out my nightmarish life when my father would sexually abuse me. I learned how to distract myself by chanting the cheers I did with Sherry in my head, louder and louder. "Blue and white, fight, fight!" and " S.U.C.C.E.S.S., that's the way we spell success!" Later I learned what I was doing was called dissociating.

When my father would finish with me, I would fade back into the reality of what had happened, roll away from the damp sheets, and bury my head in my pillow. Because I was not allowed to show any emotion, I learned to choke down my anger and swallow my tears. Finally, I would fall asleep, exhausted and depressed. Morning would come only too soon. Because I was forced to participate in my father's sin, I felt increasingly dirty and numb. I was like a robot that had no choice but to perform a dreaded duty. Each time I did, I became more and more depressed, and my enthusiasm for life waned. I knew there must be a way out, but how? My burden was extremely heavy and one I was willing to do anything to end.

Sex offenders become professionals at playing mind games with their victims, so they can easily get what they want out of them. And yes, I consider my father an expert. His life was filled with manipulative schemes to control people, which was something he learned early in life. One of his favorite tricks was to try to convince me that I was the one responsible for spurring his sexual desires. He tried to blame me for his actions. He told me again and again that it was my fault he came on to me because of the way I did my hair, the way I walked, and the way I dressed.

During my high school years, I would hurry on to school, where I would finish fixing my hair and putting on my makeup so I wouldn't "turn on" my father. I would deliberately walk stiff as a board around the house and be as unpleasant as I could. I also tried not to be seen as much as possible, but none of that worked. My father had a problem, which created enormous problems for me as well. At first, I knew no better than to believe what he told me.

But as the years progressed, I began to see through his lies as I observed his deceitful personality rolling over into other aspects of his life. I despised him and all that he did. However, I was powerless against him. He had the whip, and I was his caged pussycat. I was especially troubled because I felt I was the only one who knew how sick my father was. I wanted to scream to the world what kind of a man he was, but the shame paralyzed me from saying a word. I felt hopeless, for there was not one place for me to escape, and he delighted in reminding me of that fact. One Saturday afternoon in the summer of 1962, I was reminded how true his statement was.

I had a part-time job working at a bakery during my high school years. I came home from work smelling like grease and sweet rolls, so I would draw a bath and bathe while I listened to my favorite radio station. The warm water felt heavenly, relaxing my tired legs, and I often fell into a light sleep. Suddenly I was awakened by a "click." I opened my eyes and there was my father looking at me as if he were the devil himself. He had unlocked the bathroom door. He came in and locked the door behind him. I immediately cried out at him. "Can't you let me take a bath alone? Please go away!" I buried my face in a pile of soap bubbles.

He snorted back, "You can never lock me out, ever, so don't try this again!" He came close, knelt down and started to reach for me in the water when we heard my mother call from downstairs, "Martin, pick up the phone. Wesley wants to talk with you."

His reply to me was, "I will see you later." I knew only too well what that meant...another difficult, short night with the devil himself.

Because of the sexual acts that were forced upon me, I learned far too early adult sexual behaviors. Until then, I didn't have any idea oral sex existed, whether performed on a woman or a man. I was so grossed by his demands that I thought he must be crazy, and of course in some ways he was.

From my earliest memory of the sexual abuse, up to the age of thirteen, my father would expose himself naked and insist that he see me naked as well. I was denied privacy or a voice in any matter. I was required to allow him to see and touch me on demand. Every morning, as I began to dress for the day, he would look into our bedroom and see if I was alone. If I was, he would begin his morning ritual. His repulsive touch and morning breath was all over my body, including my mouth, for he would insist on kissing me with his mouth open. I felt filthy and humiliated before my day even began. Besides, the time he took made me late so I would have to skip breakfast just to get to school on time. I remember how my stomach would growl all morning. While I washed the supper dishes, my father would put his hand up my skirt to feel if I was having my period or not. I was constantly reminded that my life and body was not my own, and that he was the head of the household and could do anything he wanted. His brainwashing and black whip kept me a prisoner.

He admitted to me during a counseling session years later that he used my formative years to program me to be his sex playmate. Those early years were used to prepare me for what would come later. His plan was to make me obedient, so when the time came, I would tolerate his demands with little resistance. His efforts worked, for I was scared to death of his authority, strength, and black belt. Whenever he would snap his fingers, that was a signal for me to get on my knees in front of him. Then he would ask me to untie and remove his shoes. He was always looking for tasks that would remind me that I was subservient and powerless. He would tell me that I was just a simple girl, and that anything I said or thought was meaningless.

40   *Shirley Jo Petersen*

At fourteen, my father made me strip naked—but now it was in his bedroom, because mine was too frequently occupied. I had to stand there, usually in the cold air, while he stared at me and ran his clammy fingers over my tender body. Then he ordered me to turn circles for him. Totally humiliated, I would slowly turn as I covered my eyes while begging to put my clothes back on. The embarrassment was unbearable. I was completely demoralized. I was self-conscious about my lean physique and small bust-line, so shy I couldn't take showers with the other girls in gym class. To have him gawk at me and smell me while he would spread my legs and touch every part of my body was horrible. He continued to make me kiss him on his wet mouth. I would squirm and remain stiff as a board and hold my lips tight so as not to let his tongue in my mouth. Oh, how I hated him. He evoked feelings I never experienced before. Just the disgusting brushes of his mustache on my tender skin made me feel sick. He took every opportunity possible to invade my privacy and was never concerned with my feelings, or my emotional and physical health.

What stopped my father from forcing penetration earlier in my youth was lack of privacy. I shared a bedroom with three sisters and a young brother. Naomi and I slept in one double bed and my twin sisters in another across from us. My brother Benjamin's bed was under the dormer in the front of the room. When I was fifteen, my older sister Naomi moved to Grand Rapids, Michigan, to study radiology. That left the double bed all to me, or so I thought. That is when my father began initiating oral sex, which soon progressed to penetration.

I will always remember the first time he forced intercourse, for that, unfortunately, is one memory that is extremely difficult to forget. Once again, in the middle of the night he woke me with his demands to have oral sex. While I was half asleep, he would drag my hips to the side of the bed, and strip off my layers of night clothing to perform oral sex on me. I was waiting for him to finish so I could go back to sleep when I saw him stand up and lean over me. I panicked. I could see what he was about to do.

I yelled, "Stop!" Quickly, I arched my back and turned to get out of position. I gripped the bottom sheet while pushing with my feet against the bed frame trying desperately to get away from him. He grabbed my hips and wouldn't let me go.

I cried again, "No! Stop, stop!" My cry awakened my twin sisters, who were ten at the time. In the dark, Ginger bravely asked, "Dad, what are you doing to Shirley?" Abruptly, he told her to go back to sleep. Georgia and Ginger hovered silently under their bed sheets hoping he would never do to them what he was doing to me.

Once he finished with me, he turned and left, leaving my legs to dangle over the side of the bed, cold and shaking. Again, I silenced my emotions and swallowed my tears. In the darkness, I struggled to find my pajamas, and then I pulled the blankets snuggly over my head and tried to go back to sleep. That shocking experience was a dark moment in my history. Sadly, there would be more episodes to come.

My father realized I could become pregnant, so he resisted intercourse part of the time, satisfying himself with the oral sex. This was a very shameful and degrading time in my life, as you can imagine, and it is extremely difficult to be this explicit or find words that describe the emotional pain I was experiencing.

My father's abuse stripped away my dignity, and his conditioning left me helpless, with no way to protect myself. He was the king of his castle—the authoritarian— and we were to be his obedient and submissive servants. His position allowed him to do anything he wanted in his household. He abused not only me, but also the privileges he was given as a father and husband.

Many have asked where my mother was all this time. Some say she had her head buried in the sand. I answer by saying she was in "La La Land". That's the expression we children used when we saw our mom escape from a situation she could not handle. Occasionally, she would throw her hands up in the air, shake her head, and cry, "Honestly, I wish I could just fly out of here!" So many times, right along with her, I wished I could fly out of there too!

Through the years, I would frequently beg my mother for help. I would implore her to tell my father not to bother me, or touch my butt and breast, or kiss me on the mouth. I didn't know the words to describe all else he was doing. I cried, "Please have him stop. I can't stand it."

One afternoon, while my mother was stirring a pot of chili, I was once again begging for help. She took the spoon out of the large stainless steel kettle, looked straight at me and said, "Shirley, what am I to do? This is enough. Don't ever come to me with this again. I never want to hear about this and I mean it." Her response devastated me. I was sixteen at the time, and I had never felt so alone or abandoned in my life. I was like an orphaned child, and I had lost hope of having her help me out of this horrible situation.

With my head and shoulders dragging, I slowly walked away from my mother and out of the kitchen. I realized then, if I were ever to get out of this hell, I would have to do it myself. But how? From that time on, my energy was spent planning ways to escape from my father, and I knew it would be a difficult task.

My shrewd father had covered all his bases. He reminded me over and over that he was the most respected man in town. He had a certain charm, and not only was the reverend of the largest church in town, but also had a weekly devotional spot on a radio station in Kalamazoo. He told me that he had already informed the local police that I was a rebellious daughter who would say anything to get him in trouble. He ingrained in my head that if I ever told a boyfriend or husband some day, it would be the end of that relationship, for no one would want a "used rag". He would also say, "Do you know how much it would crush your mother if she knew about it, and what would happen to the family? She has no way of supporting the family, and what about the disgrace it would bring to the church if you ever told anyone? What about the embarrassment to you? You'd be marked *damaged goods* forever."

It was a huge guilt trip he laid on me. I felt as if my family's happiness, as well as the church's reputation, was contingent upon my silence. His repeated use of those piercing words made me wonder if I would ever get away.

I knew, if I was to survive, I had to do something. Out of my desperation, I dreamed up a few plans to escape from my father.

The first plan was to write letters to my Grandma and Grandpa Lillie and ask them if I could come and live with them. My Grandma and Grandpa Stone were retired and lived in a tiny travel trailer in Florida, so it was out of the question for me to live with them. In my letters, I couldn't bring myself to tell them the real reason. Instead, I told them that my father and I didn't get along, and I needed a break from him. I waited and waited for an answer, but none came. Later, I learned my Grandfather Lillie was having an ongoing relationship with his receptionist and certainly did not want a granddaughter in the way.

Plan B was to try and get pregnant by my boyfriend Loren. We would get married, and I thought that, even though I was only 16, things would probably work out. At least I would be free from my father. He was a very nice young guy who had no idea of my plan. I allowed things to get out of hand. He was the sensible one who kept saying we should cool it, because I might get pregnant, but I stayed firm on my course. I thought that getting pregnant by my boyfriend would be a situation I could live with, but getting pregnant by my father would kill me.

My plan was working well. I was about two weeks late on my period one month, and my father knew it. He was not aware of my sexual involvement with my boyfriend or my plan. All he knew was that I might be pregnant and he could be the father, since he never used any form of birth control. Little did I know he was already making plans for a possible abortion in New York State. To validate the pregnancy, I had to give him a urine sample for a pregnancy test, which he told the doctor was my mother's. The test came back negative. I wasn't pregnant. What I learned from that experience was that, even if I got pregnant, my father would not let me stay pregnant, so plan B would have to be scrapped. I ended the relationship with Loren without ever telling him the truth about our relationship or about the incest. I had to learn to live with another sad part of my story, how I hurt a kind young man. He was a true friend to me, and one I loved like a brother. Loren came to my rescue many times and provided hours of comfort to a desperate teenager in trouble.

Next was Plan C, which was to use the money I stole from my boss and escape. This plan was the ultimate scheme that opened my door to freedom.

During my high school years, I worked at a bakery. My boss Willie Riley was not only an excellent baker; he had a great zest for life, and a heart as big as all of Michigan. His business had the reputation of being the best bakery in southern Michigan, and people would drive many miles to taste his delicacies. He was a refreshing, normal male figure in my life, and gave my sister Naomi and me jobs during our high school years. He also gave us any leftover baked goods at the end of the day to take home to the family, which my Mom and siblings loved.

One Memorial Day weekend after work, Willie flew me in his single engine plane to Big Rapids to meet up with my family. That was my very first airplane ride, and he let me take the handles and navigate the plane. It was so exciting. My parents had built a rustic cabin on the Muskegon River just south of Big Rapids, and we would often go there for some R & R. My boss treated me like family and trusted me just the same. I hated myself for stealing money from the till, but somehow my yearning for money overcame my guilt. Little by little, quarter-by-quarter, I would stuff coins in my shoe and walk home with them. Gradually, I had collected more than $450 in quarters (that's about $2,500 in today's value). My plan was to take much more, but my father's actions forced me to make my move earlier than I had planned.

(A note about the stolen money: I used it to pay the tuition for nursing school two years later. However, the guilt for stealing the money was killing me, so in 1968, I returned a check to my boss for the entire amount, plus interest. I never told him all the circumstances that surrounded the stolen money but at least I paid him back, which helped to clear my conscience and allowed me to put that part of my grief to rest.

Upon receiving the check, my boss wrote me a heartwarming letter. In it, he thanked me for the money and appreciated my honesty. Willie also said he forgave me, and as far as he was concerned, my sin would never be remembered again. What a kind man.)

With the fall of 1963 came the annual homecoming festival in our little city, and one of the big events was the "Miss Plainwell" queen contest. It was the custom for any of the girls who wished to join in the fun to try out for the coveted crown. Nearly all the girls in school that I hung with were entering the contest, so I decided to as well.

My neighbor Sherry and I enjoyed shopping for the special dress and all the extra primping the contest required. We took lessons on how to walk a runway in high-heel shoes. We learned to pivot and pause, all with a queenly posture. Sherry was a beautiful girl with naturally curly hair, but it was fashionable at that time to have puffy straight hair, so she would lay her hair on the ironing board while I would try to iron it flat for her. (It didn't work well, so I don't advise trying it.)

I never told my father I was entering the contest, for I was afraid he wouldn't allow it, but my mother knew.

The exciting evening finally arrived, and after the contestants did all the parading, it was time to hear the judge's final decision.

"And the new 1963 Miss Plainwell is number 21, Shirley Jo Lillie."

"Oh, golly, that's me!" I beamed as I stepped forward to receive my honors. The applause echoed throughout the little village as the previous year's queen put a brilliant rhinestone crown on my head. The president of the chamber of commerce looped the official Miss Plainwell sash over my shoulders, and the mayor placed a fragrant bouquet of velvety red roses in my arms. Each of them offered their words of congratulations and a gentle kiss. All the queenly paraphernalia made me feel like I was truly a queen, and for the first time in my life, I felt beautiful and special.

The cool autumn evening was filled with bright camera flashes and hugs. For several wonderful hours, I had forgotten my shameful secret. That night, I had been selected to be a queen and to represent our little village for an entire year, and I would proudly do just that.

Being chosen queen was the most positive event that had ever happened to me. It elevated my self-worth and became a constant reminder that I was somebody special in spite of what my father had done to me. It was the reinforcement I desperately needed to pursue my course to freedom.

The evening's activities went by too quickly, for it was soon time to shed my rhinestone crown and satin gold gown and head for home. The following day would be busy, with a parade through town and a radio interview. As I took my gown off the hook in the dressing room and carefully folded it over my arm, I said goodnight to those who had helped me. I stepped outside into the cool, clear September night air. The streets and parking lots were now empty and ghostly quiet, and as my eyes met the stars in the heavens, I began to pray, "Oh, God, are you there? I wish I didn't have to go home tonight. Please don't let my father rape me, especially tonight!" I was on such a high, and going home meant that I had to go back to the reality of my secret, disgusting life. It was late; I thought perhaps my father would be asleep. Oh, how I hoped so. No matter what, I knew I had to face whatever was before me. Deep down, I felt like a queen and very special. No matter what my father would do to me, I was determined not to let him destroy my newly found self-worth. I was now more determined than ever to get away from him, no matter what the cost.

My time at school was a very positive experience, and I enjoyed my popularity with students and staff alike. I was a cheerleader, on the tennis team, a class officer, and on the student council. One day in junior English, while we were quoting Thomas Paine's "These are the times that try men's souls," I received a message over the intercom to come to the office. As I gathered up my books, I received looks from my peers as if to say, "What did you do now?" I wondered the same thing as I made my way down the hall to the principal's office. As I breezed around the corner, I could see a figure all too familiar leaning against the counter. I held my breath and froze momentarily.

School, so far, had been a safe place for me. I eagerly looked forward to getting away from my house and going there. It was a fun haven where I was treated with respect. In that safe environment, I felt like a normal teenager, but now my father had invaded my safe place. I slowly walked into the principal's office and faced my father. If looks could kill, he would have been dead.

Mr. Putter, the principal, said to me, "Shirley, your father has told me your mother isn't feeling well, and you are needed at home to help her, so I am excusing you for the rest of the afternoon." My stomach knotted, and my heart pounded. I knew my mom wasn't sick. She was out of town at a church meeting.

I realized then how low my father would go and to whom he would lie in order to get to me. My father was seizing the opportunity to take advantage of me once again. I slowly gathered my things from my hall locker and walked out of the school building with my father. Because of my earlier brainwashing, I felt I had no choice but to go with him. Besides, I was too ashamed to tell anyone about the incest. That day, I swore to myself this would never happen to me again. Never! Oh, how I wished I had my stolen cash with me so I could have run away. I had finally reached the point where my courage matched my anger. That evening, before I went to bed, I made a promise to myself that the next time my father approached me for sex, I would outfox him and escape. And luckily, it happened that following Saturday afternoon.

That particular Saturday, I was up cleaning my area of the bedroom. It was very quiet in the house, and I was enjoying just being alone. My twin sisters were across the street playing at a friend's house, and my mom was getting her hair done. I knew my father had gone to Kalamazoo on a hospital call, so I felt comfortable. Normally, I was terrified to be in the house alone. I had just finished hanging up all my clothes in the closet when I heard my bedroom door click open. I looked up, thinking it was one of my sisters, but it wasn't. It was my father, who had come home early. I was scared to death. My chest felt like I was suffocating. I had told him so many times before, if he touched me again, it would be the last time and I'd be out of there. But this time was different, because I really meant it, and I finally had the funds to help me carry out my threat. He started to approach me, and as he did, I gasped, "No! Leave me alone. I told you if you ever touched me again, I was out of here, and I mean it this time." I suddenly turned and jumped over the twins' double bed, and then quickly slipped out the doorway. It happened so fast, my father's lunge for me was a miss. By now I was gasping, but I kept running, fearful my father was right on my tail. The warm tears flooded my eyes, and I struggled to see the stair steps that led to the main floor, but I kept going. When I got to the bottom of the stairs, I swung open the front door, jumped down the two front cement steps and started running full speed toward town. I was overwhelmed with fear and uncertainty, but I knew I must clear my head and start planning my next move.

The brisk afternoon air filled my lungs, and with every breath, I felt a surge of new energy. As I ran, I wiped my tears with my sleeve, and then for some reason looked up at the sky. Above me was the most beautiful, clear, turquoise blue heaven I had ever seen. And just ahead of me flew a tiny sparrow. It was then I realized the immensity of what I had just done. I had escaped. I really did it! I was as free as that bird that seemed to be leading me on. There would never be any more horrible midnight invasions. I had a vibrant sense of accomplishment. If only I had packed an overnight bag or grabbed my coat. Oh well, at least I was free at last!

I hated the prospect of having to quit school, but I knew that was a definite possibility in order for me to support myself. My mind raced; maybe my boss would hire me full-time and let me stay in the bakery basement, or I could take a bus to Kalamazoo or Grand Rapids and find work there.

Back in the '60s, there were no women's shelters or crisis centers, and certainly no place for a runaway teenager as exist today. I was totally on my own and desperate for help.

While running down the block, I searched for the best plan. School would be out in a couple of months, and the prom was coming up. I had a date with a young man I was crazy about. I had also planned to attend college, but that, too, would have to be scrapped if I did not graduate from high school. I was in a real dilemma as to what to do next.

I had finally settled into a comfortable walk when I heard footsteps behind me. I hesitated to look but my curiosity got the best of me. I turned my head for a quick glance. It was the one face that I feared the most. My father called out to me and said he wanted to talk. As he spoke, I immediately began to pick up speed. Again he called out, "Please listen to me." I realized he was staying a fair distance away so I stopped and dared to listen for a moment. As he began to talk, for the first time in my life, I saw my father frightened. He knew I was serious this time about leaving. He realized his career and life were in jeopardy by what I was going to do next, and that his threats and lies could no longer hold me captive. I listened cautiously to what he had to say. He promised that if I came home, he would never touch me again, and had gone so far as to write it on a piece of paper as a promissory note for me to keep. I was extremely leery of his promise, for he had used that technique to coerce me into having sex with him before, including giving me notes, which he would always confiscate later. Time and time again, he would say, "This will be the last time." But it never was. He also promised that he would never touch my twin sisters either, for he knew that was one thing I feared might happen if I left. Luckily, the twins had each other, and they were constantly together. I knew it would be harder for him to get to them.

Did I dare believe him after so many lies? I told him I would think about it but gave him no promises, and then I added, " If I do come back, and you break your word, I will shout it loud from your pulpit and let the whole world know what you have been doing to me!" My pride had totally vanished. I didn't care anymore what people might think. I was hesitant, but snatched the hand-written note. (Unfortunately, this also disappeared, for he stole it back from me a week later. He searched until he found my secret hiding place. I had tacked it to an inside wall panel in a tiny crawl space behind my twin sisters' bed.)

My father turned and walked home. I watched him from a distance until he walked out of sight, then I proceeded on my way. I continued to walk, considering my options that afternoon. I finally concluded that I would be risking too much if I did not return home and try it one last time.

When I reached home, my mother asked me what I had done all afternoon. I told her I was with Sherry. That evening, as the family gathered for supper, no one had the slightest clue as to what had transpired earlier between my father and me. After my father said the blessing, I began to pick at my food and never once looked up at his face. I was frightened, and desperately hoped that I had made the right decision.

The Ultimate Betrayal"

A father's betrayal
Leaves a brand of its own
A scar too deep
To let it be known

We hide and pretend
That all is well
The shame we embody
Is too painful to tell

The brand burns still
Though covered by years
For a father's betrayal
Is the worst there is

The Whisper 53

ABOVE: Shirley's family in
1959.
RIGHT: Shirley, Queen of
Plainwell.
BELOW: Cheerleader
Shirley, standing on right.

4

Refuse to be continually victimized.

The sidewalk conversation with my father in the spring of 1964 was monumental, as was the decision to return home that afternoon. I hardly slept a wink that first night, fearing the worst would happen, but it didn't. Nor did it happen the next night or the next. Thus began the start of a whole new chapter in my life, one of hiding a huge dark family secret and of trying to get on with my life.

After I was convinced that the sexual abuse had stopped, I tried to forget it ever happened. I desperately wanted to put it out of mind; however, living in the same house, day after day, with the man who had sexually abused me made it extremely difficult. Once the sexual abuse stopped, I thought things would be better. Unfortunately, that wasn't so. The atmosphere at home was still very unpleasant. My father disliked having lost control of the situation and continued to make my life difficult. He constantly gave me vicious stares and sly, mean remarks in private. The anxiety from his treatment literally made me ill, but at least he was out of my bed, and I was able to graduate from high school. I could hardly wait to be able to support myself and be out on my own. And what about my date for the prom? Well, I went to the prom, and that special, handsome man became my husband a little more than two years later.

If you were raised in the mid to late 1960s, you may remember the actress Julie Andrews. She starred in the 1964 musical *The Sound of Music*. In that movie, she had a particularly striking line, a reminder that we need to face our problems, for we cannot run away from them. At eighteen, I let that advice go right over my head, for I was a senior in high school and trying hard to forget that incest had ever happened. I was anxiously trying to get on with my life and was using denial as a way of erasing my unpleasant memories.

I finally realized that denial doesn't work. I did not understand it then, but that approach only made my life worse and contributed to further problems.

Author Melody Beatty claims that denial is the shock absorber of the soul and protects us until we are ready to face the really hard stuff. Denial was a form of coping that provided me with more than just time. It also gave me a false sense of comfort.

One thing that surprised me was that, as the years went by, the more the sexual abuse troubled me. You would think it would be just the opposite, but that wasn't so. Time did not soften its blow. The more I began to comprehend just how much my sordid past had negatively affected my life and my family's, the more angry I became with my abuser. Yet, because of my conditioning, and the lies my father had planted in my head years earlier, I didn't dare take my problem to anyone for help. My horrendous shame chained me to that silence. I think only another victim of incest can understand the amount of humiliation and emotional pain you feel after such degrading acts have been done to you—especially when the predator was your own father. And my father, being a minister, only added to my humiliation, for he was supposed to hold to a higher standard. That is why I refer to my incest experience as the ultimate betrayal.

For the following twenty-five years, I tried to cover up my wounds. I used patch upon patch and lie upon lie to avoid the ugly story, until I could no longer play that game. We have all heard the old saying, "Oh, what a tangled web we weave when first we practice to deceive." The deceitful part of my life was what really tore at my heart, especially when it involved the one person whom I loved the most, my husband. For, from the beginning of our marriage, Jim believed that our relationship was built on honesty. We shared all the events of our past, all except for my experience with incest. Jim often questioned why I came to bed wearing layers of night clothing and underwear, and why I resisted intimacy. I just told him I was cold or tired. After years of marriage, Jim concluded that the problem of our physical intimacy must be a result of his inadequacies as a man. That was so far from the truth, and I could not allow Jim to take the blame any longer for what my father had done to me in my youth. The real problem in our relationship was that I was a victim of incest and incapable of sharing that critical truth with my husband or anyone else. Because of that, serious problems developed.

An important truth I finally came to understand is that when we harbor hate and hide hideous secrets, we allow ourselves to be continually victimized. *This greatly injures us, not our perpetrators.* They aren't even aware of our private torment, nor do they care. The mental torture and physical ailments that we receive from our private anguish only produce more suffering, causing our cycle of pain to continue.

This is *not* how I dreamed my life would be, controlled by my past. In fact, I was determined as a teenager to have a wonderful life in spite of it. After all I went through, I felt I deserved it. However, untying the knots that bound me to my past became an impossible task, regardless of my best efforts. I had far too many hang-ups and too little knowledge to overcome my nagging problems.

Dr. Robert Schuller, the world-renowned speaker and television minister, coined a great quote when he said, "Capitalize on your pain. Turn your pain into something that can be of some benefit to you."

The thought of turning my emotional pain into something from which I could benefit sounded outrageous. What could I possibly gain from being a victim of incest? Yet I cautiously proceeded with that idea out of the sheer determination not to let my incest experience destroy another day of my life or my husband's. I was hungry for suggestions on how to improve my life, so I read, watched TV talk shows—and yes, even listened to sermons—yet all their advice seemed unattainable. I learned from one of Dr. Schuller's sermons that I needed to be willing to *let go* of my righteous hatred towards my abuser and find ways to turn my pain into gain, whatever that could be. At that time in my life I interpreted "to let it go" was the same as "to forgive" and I was not about to do that. I felt my father was deserving of every bit of my hate; besides, those hateful feelings gave me some justifiable pleasure, and somehow compensated for the horror he put me through. However, I also understood—especially the nurse in me— what hate can do to a person. I was already feeling the negative effects from it, and I was far away from the wonderful life I had always dreamed of having.

There were many times during the following 25 years that I recalled Dr. Schuller's words, "Capitalize on your pain. Turn your pain into something that can be of some benefit."

His message planted a seed in my heart, and from that seed grew courage to eventually begin writing *The Whisper*.

5

Are all families dysfunctional to some degree?

The emotional abuse we children experienced while growing up began as early as I can remember. Our father's need for power and control led him to overpower those within his household—including my mother—both physically and emotionally. He articulated his words and moves in such a manner as to control and force us into obedience. My father seemed to enjoy seeing our fearful submission, and if we dared to disobey, our punishments far exceeded our crimes.

One evening, while my sister Naomi and I were sleeping, I was awakened by her cries. My father was pulling her out of bed by her hair and taking her down to the kitchen to rewash the supper dishes because she had left water spots on some of the glasses. She was only seven at the time. He took all of the dishes out of the cupboard and made her wash them before she could go back to bed. Our father required perfection out of Naomi and gave everything she did the "white glove test". (Later, I learned that he was replaying what his father had done to him so many years ago.)

My father's motto was "children (if you had to have them at all) were to be seen and not heard". Father was to be served first always, and what he said went. If anyone disagreed with him, they would have a meeting with "Mr. Black." Mr. Black was very real in our house, and he got used often, especially on my older siblings. It was a black barber strap used for sharpening blades. My father found that his sharpening belt made a handy tool for paddling his children. He also carved a handle in a flat board to use for spanking as a variation. He would not hesitate to use these tools to punish us. He was determined to put the fear of God in us through him.

Our oldest brother David received the brunt of our father's wrath. He was three years older than I, and my memory tells me that he was always being whipped for something; either wetting the bed or forgetting to do something he was supposed to do. While David was being whipped, I watched our mother bury her face in her apron and cry, "Oh, David, David, I feel so bad!" Yet, she would not or could not stop the lickings. Being the oldest, David carried a huge load. Even as a young lad, David was sensitive to our mother's physical needs and helped her with the domestic chores. He took the role of the surrogate father and protector, not a role he necessarily liked, but one he knew he must take. During those years, even as a youngster, my heart hurt for him, for I was instinctively aware of his heavy physical and emotional load. I watched David and Naomi try to do their best for our father. Unfortunately, it seldom seemed good enough. Naomi's spunky nature and quick tongue often got her into trouble. Yet, her strong personality also saved her from the trouble I found myself in. Years later, my father told me that Naomi's strong willed nature would not allow him to get away with any form of sexual abuse. He also said that I was picked very young to take that role as he noted my more compliant nature. How could I be anything else, as I saw the whippings my siblings received?

Our father was a strong dictator, and getting his own way was critical for him. His lust for power and prestige were the biggest reasons he remained a minister. For him, the "Reverend" in front of his name was a power trip, as he thrived on the authority it gave him. It helped to fill a hole that was left from the wounds of his childhood. Later, he confided to me that being a pastor was the worst occupation he could have ever pursued. He confessed that the authority it gave him provided opportunities to misuse that power.

A common way my father vented his anger was on the highway. The term "road rage" was coined for people like my father. He had a dangerous lead foot and often would recklessly cross several lanes in front of oncoming traffic, or would pass on the right shoulder of the road.

Back in the 1950s, my father accidentally killed a lady with his car. He hit her when she darted in front of him while crossing the street. You would think that would have slowed him down, but not so.

My mother was terrified to ride with him. She would call me even after I was married and cry, "Honestly, Shirley, your father is going to kill us both some day with his reckless driving. I can't stand to ride with him anymore. He's making me a nervous wreck!"

Whenever she did say anything about his driving, he would rebuke her, swatting at her and saying, "Shut up, Adel!" I also feared his careless driving would kill them both one day.

And of course, my father was often stopped for speeding. When this happened, he tried to talk his way out of the ticket. He would say boastfully to the officer, "Listen, officer, I'm Reverend Martin Lillie, a minister of the Gospel!" as though he should receive immunity because of his title.

The policeman would reply, " I don't care who you are, Mister. You were breaking the law and here is your ticket!" My father would respond indignantly. We children would scrunch down in our seats with embarrassment.

We children were exposed to many similar situations that were unhealthy while growing up. I have learned that it takes a lifetime to undo the twisted lessons I learned in my childhood. Many I thought were okay, because that is all I knew, such as how you casually use people, exaggerate the truth, or put on an air of importance. I have many regrets in those areas, and yet I've learned to let them go and to put my energy into just doing better. I heard a speaker say that this life is just a dress rehearsal for the next. If that's so, I'm practicing hard so I will do much better in the next.

The public saw a different man than the one that lived at our house. My father put on a good front and knew how to impress those who sat in the pews. His scriptural emphasis was often on fearing God and submission. Wives were to submit to their husbands and children were to obey and do what they were told, regardless. And if we didn't, parents were not to spare the rod. He also stressed staying sexually pure. Yeah, right!

One afternoon, my father pointed out to me a particular story in the Old Testament. It was about a father who gave his virgin daughter over to the invading soldiers. It was a brutal account of how she was sexually abused and then thrown on her parents' doorstep when they finished with her. My father wanted to prove to me that there were other daughters who had it a lot worse, so I should stop complaining about what he was doing to me.

It would be years later before I would hear sermons from another pastor on faith, hope and love—and the greatest of these is love—and how much God hates evil, and that children were gifts from God to be loved like God loves us.

My father fulfilled his job requirements by visiting the sick, performing marriage ceremonies, and offering comforting words to those grieving. To the community, he was pleasant and always looked professional in his dark suit, white starched shirt and tie, and black slicked down hair. For those who didn't really know him, it was easy to be fooled by the man in black who lived at our house.

My parents claimed they had two different groups of children within the seven. I believe we first three felt the full force of my father's physical and emotional abuse. However, I have to admit I received fewer spankings than my two older siblings. I learned quickly from their examples what to do and what not to do. The last four children describe their abuse by our father as more of abandonment. However, they too met up with Mr. Black. We did not know what a warm or healthy relationship with a father could be. He spoke to us when it was for his own good or to rebuke us. I saw his contacts as cool and impersonal. The name "Heavenly Father" referring to God our Father was not one that brought me any comfort. My negative image of what a father was became a barrier in understanding the biblical truth about God our loving Heavenly Father.

While growing up, how hungry we children were— especially we girls—to hear the words "I love you", or to receive a hug or an encouraging word from our father, but it just never happened. He told us girls to stop primping because we were just average and no amount of primping could help. We desperately needed a father's love and affirmation, and, because we didn't receive it, we went elsewhere looking for it, whether to our boyfriends or girlfriends, teachers, neighbors, or co-workers. We hungrily absorbed any special attention and approval others gave us, and as a result, we became easy prey for outside influences and further abuse.

I still remember my friends hesitating before coming into our house when my father was inside because of the unpleasant aura he presented. Whenever I would ask a friend to come in, they would ask, "Is your father at home?" When I answered yes, they'd say, "No, let's play outside or go over to my house." My best friend Kay called her parents to come and get her because the atmosphere was scary—so much so that she didn't want to be around him. Besides, there were no books, bikes, or toys to play with in our house.

As a youngster, I couldn't help but notice the different atmosphere in other households. Their family relationships were odd yet intriguing. I began to realize just how different ours was. I was instinctively aware that the incest was wrong, but all the other stuff was all I knew. Years later, when I learned the word "dysfunctional", I knew that was the word that described our family.

We did have one book in our house, and it was the Bible. When my father was a pastor, after supper he would read it to us and have us memorize scripture verses. He wanted to set an example to his congregation of how religious training should be done. That wasn't all bad, for we also learned to memorize the books of the Bible and that has been useful. At least that time allowed us to have some positive family interaction.

Hearing verses read in the King James Bible often triggers negative memories of my father. I have appreciated other translations of the Bible, for his voice is not so evident when I read them. Also, perhaps that is the reason the lyrics to my music have been so comforting.

*"Oh, yes, I know who I am, and I'm privileged to say
I'm a child of God, loved by Him, always.
Although storms of life try to whip me about
I'm held secure in God's loving arms."*

It is a tragedy for children when there is no one to protect them from abuse. Because of that void, they become vulnerable to more abuse throughout their lifetimes. They don't realize they are worthy of any different treatment. Consequently, they naturally accept what comes along until they learn differently. Hopefully, they will.

My father, the one who was supposed to be my protector, became the villain, my abuser. And my mother, who was also supposed to protect me, abandoned me in my time of greatest need. I was in a very tough place at a difficult time in my life. Growing up in that environment left me with many social and emotional handicaps. By my mother's example I learned to accept abuse, tolerate wrongs, stay silent, and fake a happy life if you have to. I believe my mother's philosophy came from the wrongful indoctrination she received from her spiritual leaders. She literally believed what she was taught in 2nd Corinthians, chapter 13: "Love bears *all* things." If she questioned my father, she was rebuked for not being a submissive wife. She was not allowed to think otherwise or to combat the wrong that was evident in our household. If she did, she was scolded for being disobedient. Because of her example and the same brainwashing I received, I never learned to protect or defend myself. That is one of the reasons it took me so long to break from my abusive situation.

When I became a mother, I found it difficult to even defend my children in emotionally abusive situations. I didn't have the tools or self-confidence to do otherwise. Luckily, my strong, six foot six husband jumped to the plate. His understanding of what is right and wrong made it instinctive for him to react in a healthy manner. His example has been and still is a tremendous help to his family.

It has taken years to overcome my abusive, submissive conditioning and develop a strong sense of self-worth. And I continue to work on it. I know I am much stronger, and if you ask my husband and family, they would wholeheartedly agree. (More on how I accomplished this is further on.)

6

*Blood relation does not always mean
you are thick as blood.*

The greatest gifts my parents gave to me are my six siblings: David, Naomi, Joshua, Georgia, Ginger, and Benjamin. I was not fully aware of that until my adult years. Unlike a lot of other families, I was not raised to appreciate, support, or love them like I should have. My husband was instrumental in showing me how families are supposed to support one another. I remember one occasion when my brother Joshua was running cross-country in high school. He had an important track meet, and Jim said, "Let's go. We need to be there for him." He told my parents they should be there also. They were surprised by Jim's insistence. It wasn't until Jim's remark that I questioned the absence of my parents at my school events. I was a cheerleader for four years, on the varsity tennis team for four years, and received awards on many occasions, but my parents were always absent. Occasionally I would ask them to come but their response was always that they were busy doing God's work. Their lack of interest in my activities only reinforced my lack of importance. You would think, being raised in a so-called

Christian home, that love and support for family would be the first thing taught to us. For isn't that how we learn about God's love, by being supported and nurtured in a loving family environment? But then again, our household emphasis was not on love or grace, but rather on fear and the law.

For years, I didn't think my brothers or sisters liked me, so how could I possibly go to them with my most secret problem? We all lived under the same roof, but in many ways, we lived very isolated lives from each other because we didn't know how else to live.

However, breaking the news of the incest started a whole new kinship between us. It immediately broke down the walls of indifference, and we began to verbalize our individual grievances. As I exposed my father's sexual sins, other family members braved telling their heartaches. It was painful to admit how dysfunctional our family was, as well as to learn of our father's sexual sins. We once saw ourselves coming from a respected, prominent family. Now that had crumbled. At that time, we were all married with children of our own. We were facing the sad realization that some of the unhealthy examples we had learned had trickled down into our own family interactions. That painful awareness began needed improvements.

Each of my brothers and sisters had his or her own issues resulting from the parenting of Martin and Adel. And everyone said that opening up the family secret, although initially devastating, greatly improved her or his life in one way or another.

The initial reactions from my siblings to my shocking news were not all positive. Naomi emphatically said, "Why are you telling me this? And why do you feel you need to tell anyone? I don't need to know about it!" She had a hard time with this information, because even though our father physically and emotionally abused her, she admired our father's strength. She saw our mother as weak, and that behavior was not one she wanted to emulate. Later, Naomi was the one who said, "Shirley, I wish I had known about this much earlier. Your story would have helped me so much. I feel so terrible for you!"

My youngest sister Ginger said that my story was the last piece of the puzzle she needed to finally understand her fears as a child. Now she knew what my father was doing to me in the middle of the night, and what the upsetting whispers were all about. For her, an age-old question was finally answered.

We four sisters consider it a miracle as well as a blessing that we have developed a *love bond* for each other, considering how we were raised. It took years of us observing how other healthy families related to each other before we took hold and developed what should have been ours all along. We love getting together and taking yearly vacations. We strive to develop loving, strong ties within our families and stress the importance of having faith in God. We're not perfect families. However, we try to reflect the loveliness our maiden name represents.

In the early1980s, I shared a shortened version of my story with my oldest brother David. My father was planning to admit girls to the Christian boarding school he began. I was so convinced that he would sexually abuse the female students that I nearly went crazy. All I could think about was my father abusing those girls. At that time, David was working closely with my father, and I thought if he knew, he could make sure it never happened. The story was nearly impossible to tell, but for the safety of the girls, I knew I had to.

The conversation began while we were canoeing one summer afternoon. I said, "David, there is something you need to know about our father. He sexually abused me when I was home. And now that he is accepting girl students into the program, I'm terrified he will start to abuse them. You have to keep a close eye on him!"

David, in silence, shook his head as in disbelief. Then he said, "I had no idea, Sis." I knew he felt bad, for he had always been my protector while growing up. As we talked, he remembered incidents from the past that made my story believable. I made him swear to keep our conversation a secret. Then David asked, "Sis, when are you going to tell Jim? He needs to know." I just shook my head. I never wanted to tell my story to anyone else again—especially to my husband.

I regard my brothers and sisters each as a work of art in their own way, and I have an enormous amount of appreciation and love for each one of them. Their emotional support and understanding through this whole ordeal has been extremely helpful.

At one time, we lived under the same roof, yet we have seven different views of the events of our childhood. Because I was the only child who was sexually abused, I had an unusually difficult relationship with our father. And because the incest was hidden from the rest of the family, my story was understandably troubling to them.

Today, we siblings look forward to gathering and creating new memories. And as graduations, weddings, and vacation time arrive, we celebrate the love we share that grew out of our dysfunctional family.

My counselor told me that the outcome of my situation, the restitution and healing of my family, is what a counselor dreams of for all his clients. He also told me that what I experienced is the exception, rather than the rule. Unfortunately, my positive outcome doesn't happen frequently enough. Yet, he reminded me that one could still find healing from his or her abuse and come to a resolution in spite of a lack of family involvement.

I have been fortunate in many ways. My brothers and sisters have stood by me and supported me—and continue to do so. That is why I say the best things my parents ever gave me were my siblings.

"Stand By Me"

Stand by me and be my friend,
And help my hurting heart to mend.
For freedom I paid a mighty fee,
Still a dark lonely cloud hovers over me.

You need not say a word
But look at me as if you heard,
The quiet cries within my heart
Oh, what sadness I impart.

Stand by me, I need a friend,
One on whom I can depend.
For I've been blamed, and even shamed
For letting the truth be known.

Brothers and sisters, in birth order. Shirley is 3rd from left.

7

Are you living in a bubble and it's about to burst?

I remember how exhausting it was in my teen years to cover up for my father's sins. I was so afraid someone might suspect what he was doing to me that I would lie, or say anything to avoid telling anyone about the incest. I was *so ashamed*; I would have died if anyone knew. Even after the abuse stopped, I felt I needed to put on the disgusting act that my father and I had a good relationship. I feared if I acted out how I really felt about him, people would ask questions, and I was not about to go there.

However, shortly before Jim and I were married, my future father-in-law, Edward, picked up on something suspicious about my father. During a little pre-nuptial talk with his son, Edward expressed to Jim that he had serious concerns about my father. He said, "Jimmy, I don't know what it is, but there is something about Martin I just don't trust, so be careful. I think it is important for you to know this." My father-in-law was surprisingly intuitive.

On my wedding day, I was faced with a problem regarding the great father/daughter image I'd been faking. My father came into my dressing room and wanted to talk to me about something he thought was important. He wanted me to kiss him in front of everyone during the part of the wedding ceremony when he put my hand in Jim's.

So far, I thought I had pulled off a normal image of what a daughter and father relationship was supposed to be, but I couldn't do this. I didn't want to kiss him or even touch him on my wedding day. In no way did I want him to wreck this perfect day, but he would not leave my dressing room until I said yes. I told myself that this would be the very last time I would have to pucker up and kiss my father.

My marriage to Jim was the happiest event in my life, and I looked forward to us living a long, wonderful life together. I envisioned us having the perfect marriage, for I knew I had the perfect man. Our home would be a place where I could finally relax and begin to live a normal life like everyone else, or so I thought.

Our wedding turned out to be a very large occasion. My folks extended an open invitation to everyone in the church, and I think nearly everyone came. Luckily for us, Willie, my bakery boss, gave us a wedding cake for our wedding gift, one that was large enough to feed our 500 guests.

My wedding gown was one I borrowed from my sister-in-law Roxanne, who had worn it only two years earlier. It was a beautiful, off-white satin gown with lace inlay and a ten-foot cathedral train. It needed only slight alterations to fit. The gown was a New York original, and I felt honored to be allowed to wear it. To personalize my attire, I purchased a fingertip veil and lined the hem with small white fabric daisies.

Jim's parents provided the lovely arrays of gladiolas for the wedding ceremony. Each of the attendants carried a bouquet of pastel daisies. Daisies are still one of my favorite flowers, symbolizing resilience and freedom. Whenever I see them nodding in an open field, I reflect back to the time when I gained my freedom, and that's a wonderful memory.

The flowers for our wedding reception came from a recent funeral. My father had made arrangements with the local undertaker, who was also a member of our church, to save any flowers that were left from a funeral during that week. Obviously that is all he felt I deserved, for he had the funds to do more. My mother and my Aunt Liz did their best to make centerpieces out of the wilted buds but in spite of their best efforts, they were a sorry sight.

It was our decision to get married while we were still in college, so with our limited funds, we had little choice but to go with what was provided for us. We were happy just to be getting married, so the flower thing didn't matter much. Besides, I wasn't surprised by my father's actions. I knew he didn't think I deserved anything better.

June 11, 1965, turned out to be a perfect evening for a wedding. My little brother Benjamin was the acolyte, and once he got the candles lit (there were several attempts), the evening's magic began.

My five bridal attendants looked stunning as they proceeded down the aisle in their handmade, aqua blue brocade gowns. Through the sheer curtains at the back of the church, I peeked past the hundreds of people and saw Jim standing at the end of the long white runner. The scene looked like one from a dream, with my handsome prince standing tall in his black tux and tails, while candles flickering from behind. I was ecstatic, for my ultimate dream was about to come true. I reluctantly put my hand through my father's arm and off we went, down the aisle to greet my soon-to-be new husband.

About ten steps into the wedding march, my high-heeled shoe got tangled in the lining of my wedding gown. I heard a rip and began to trip. I struggled briefly to untangle my foot before proceeding on down the aisle. When the time came for my father to give my hand to Jim, my eyes were so focused on Jim that I truly forgot to give my father the kiss. To this day, I am glad that I had that momentary memory lapse. My father reprimanded me after the ceremony about my memory blitz, but I didn't care. I was no longer a daughter living under his roof or authority. I was proud and thankful to be Mrs. James Petersen and free from my father at last, or at least that's what I thought.

Being completely free from my father and the effects of the incest proved to be a long and difficult task, for my father continued to harass me for years. Whenever we were at family gatherings, he would quickly find me and give me a controlling hug. To others, it looked like I might be his favorite daughter. Then he would gruffly whisper in my ear, "Have you told Jim yet?" With a fake smile, I would quietly answer "No." Then he would say, "Good, because your marriage would be over if he knew, for no man wants damaged goods." Still in my fake smile, I slowly stepped away from the man I secretly hated, and now the show was over. No one suspected a thing, and my secret remained.

My father continued to call me from pay phones, to tell me that Jim wouldn't want damaged merchandise, so I'd better keep my mouth shut. His words were ingrained in my head, as were the memories of the sexual abuse. My father kept me a prisoner of my past, but my shame was the key that locked the door.

It took several years before I realized that I could have told Jim the truth from the beginning, and it would have been okay. However, I remembered one evening shortly after we were engaged, when I witnessed Jim's hatred of sexual crimes. We were watching the evening news when the commentator told a story about a man who had raped a young teen. Jim's response was; "That man should be killed. If that were my daughter, he'd be dead." He was so angry. It was then I wondered if my father would have remained alive, or if Jim's anger might have led to him going to jail if I told him. Unfortunately, for years, I was still replaying my father's lie, "You are damaged merchandise, and no one would want you if they knew."

I had a tug of war going on with my heart and my head, and my head was winning. I loved Jim so much, I didn't want to embarrass him because of what had happened to his wife, and so I stayed silent for the next twenty-five years.

During our early married years, Jim and I were able to work through the normal adjustments of married life with relative ease. We didn't require a lot of material things to make us happy. Also, our goals were the same. Most importantly, we had deep affection for each other; however, our interests were nearly opposite. Jim loved all kind of sports, as well as hunting, fishing, and playing cards. My interests were in the arts and music, and I loved to play games. Because of my example, I was a very compliant wife and demanded little. My father's early conditioning reinforced that women were to serve men, and their personal wants didn't matter.

Twenty-five years later, and well into my journey toward health, I announced to Jim that I don't liked sports, and I didn't like to play cards either. I only tolerated them for him, and I said I wasn't going to do that anymore. A new spirit of freedom had emerged. Jim looked at me, puzzled, and said, "Shirl, you've changed." I answered, "No, I've always disliked them. It's just now I'm free to verbalize my feelings and am confident enough to say and do what I want to for a change. It's time for me to be true to me."

When Jim told me that I wasn't the gal he first married, I answered by saying, "You are right. I'm better—healthier and wiser." Jim chuckled, and with a twinkle in his eye, he said, "You are really special, Shirley.

You are just lucky that I love you so much." Jim adjusted to his more vocal, changing wife, and his commitment to love me—for better or worse, has stayed true. More than anything, he's glad I'm healthy and happy.

No matter what our few differences are, I have come to realize how lucky I was to marry Jim, especially at the young age of nineteen. I maintain it was what saved me from experiencing many of the common problems incest victims face, such as promiscuity, dependency on drugs or alcohol, or other self-destructive behaviors. Our marriage provided a safe environment for me to grow in, one in which I felt safe and loved.

However, the first twenty-five years of our marriage were not healthy years for me. I had bouts of migraine headaches and depression, consequences from my sexual abuse. The light in the bathroom was the most common cause for the headaches. Whenever anyone would turn on the bathroom light in the middle of the night (which happened nearly every night), I would begin to dream my father was coming in to abuse me, for that's how it happened as a child. The light triggered a memory. Half asleep, I would see my father's shadow coming toward me, and I'd begin to shiver and wrap myself up tightly in the blanket so he couldn't get to me. When I would awaken, my head would be throbbing, and a migraine headache would soon follow.

Back in the days of the incest, I wore layers of sleep wear, including socks, underwear and button-up tops that tucked in, anything that might deter my father from abusing me. It never worked. In fact, I think he enjoyed me playing "hard to get"—only I wasn't playing.

For the first few months of marriage, I was easily distracted from the memory of my father. The wonderful effects of being a newlywed encompassed me. However, those feeling were short-lived. Eventually I began to think of my father every time Jim made any kind of sexual advance.

One evening, I remember literally hitting Jim on the head during lovemaking. He was confused and hurt by my action. I made up some story like he accidentally hurt me. It is such a relief not to have to lie any more. Even though Jim tried to please me sexually, it was next to impossible to respond naturally. I would try to fake responses the best I could, but Jim began to see through them. Through the years, he concluded that my problem must be his lack of ability to meet my sexual needs, and that falsehood is what ultimately gave me the courage to tell him about my sordid past. I loved Jim too much to allow him to take any fault for a wrong that occurred long before he entered the picture. Jim deserved to know the reason why I was so unresponsive to him, and to have a better wife than I was able to be at that time. He was naturally sensual and loving. I was the one with the problem. That evening of truth in 1991 was long overdue.

As I have alluded to earlier, a serious consequence of my sexual abuse was the inability to enjoy a sexual experience, even within the circle of a loving and committed relationship. Our sexuality is a beautiful gift when shared with a beloved, and to be robbed of that enjoyment and the closeness it brings is a tremendous loss.

Jim and I realized that we had a lot of work ahead of us if I was to overcome my sexual handicap. We were determined to conquer this problem so we could both experience the enjoyment of physical intimacy. In order for that to happen, we needed to communicate at the most intimate and truthful level possible. It became imperative for Jim to know every ugly detail of my sexual abuse, what exactly happened, what time of the day or night, in what position, and so on. By knowing all, he was able to avoid things that would trigger memories of the incest. He became creative by adding playful tender moments that kept our personal time lighthearted and fun. Jim patiently waited for me to be the one to initiate any kind of sexual intimacy. We spent many hours holding and kissing, with my layered night clothing on. Then he would whisper, "Your skin feels so much better than these clothes." Slowly, I would take out a shoulder. That was enough, and Jim didn't push for more. Eventually, feeling his wonderful warmth, and knowing how much he loved me regardless of my past, made me want to get even closer. Jim often reminded me that I could always stop, or say no, with no questions asked. His patience, insight, and persistence during this delicate time were incredible, and necessary to develop an intimate relationship, especially after incest.

Eventually, the ghost of my past left our bed, and we gained the beautiful gift God originally intended for us to have. Many times, I have thought of all the years of intimacy I wasted by not telling Jim about the incest early on. My silence was a big mistake, and one I hope others will not make.

An important factor that contributed to our sexual intimacy was the emotional intimacy we developed. We truly got into the minds and hearts of the other for the first time. The hours we spent communicating made our relationship wonderfully rich. We try hard to listen to what the heart of the other is saying and respond in a sensitive manner. That is a skill that took time and desire on both our parts to develop.

My friend Donna asked me if Jim and I ever fight. We occasionally do have disagreements, but we have learned to fight fair. We took some hard knocks until we had that skill perfected. Those arguments happened after I came out with my story, and I was strong enough to hold my own. Out of our love, we allow each other to freely disagree and to have our own opinion, and we respect each other's views. This is something neither of us saw in the examples of our parents. Even in our heated conversations, there is strength in our marriage because of all we have gone through together.

Fortunately, I married Jim because I really loved him, not just to escape from my situation. Two other young men had previously asked me to marry them, and although it was tempting, I couldn't because I didn't love them.

Jim's love continues to be my most treasured gift, and I would never want to be with out it. I cherish him now more than ever. Today, our biggest disagreement is a heartwarming one: which one loves the other the most. A bit sappy, I know!

A woman in a class I conducted expressed that she thought it was easier for Jim to love me and handle my abuse problems than it is for most men, and I agreed with her.

Jim came into our marriage with very little baggage. He brought a heart that was free to love me completely. He is also a very unselfish man. I am his number one concern and he has devoted his life to putting me first. He believes caring for me is his God given purpose. He thinks it is every husband's purpose as well, when they choose to marry. He believes men should be willing to lay down their life for their wife. He not only saw this example in his Dad, but also found it to be Biblical.

I know I am very lucky and I thank God for Jim every day. I still believe Jim is God's gift to me to make up for the abuse in my youth. I feel God's love so profoundly through Jim. Jim made it possible for me to trust and love God again. Love is so important, especially the agape love that God gives. It transforms and heals lives.

I believe every woman and man can learn to love deeply and unselfishly. That power comes when we get in touch with the *Creator of Love*, and allow God's love to enter us and change us into the person we want to be.

Several years ago, Jim began to do something important to prove his love for me. Whenever he is watching television and I come into the room to speak to him, he immediately looks at me and mutes the TV, even when sports are on. Now that shows real love, for he loves his sports. Love is an action word, that's for sure.

I once heard a minister say that the wedding of the couple takes place on that special day they chose to get married, but the real marriage of their hearts takes place some twenty years or more down the road. I believe that is true, but if there are dark secrets between the couple, it will never happen—take it from me. If anyone wants a truly intimate relationship with another, you need to share all of yourself—no holding back.

It takes a long time for two hearts to mold together as one, no matter how clean your background may be. Let's face it; women and men are wired differently. We often process things differently, which frequently causes conflict. A friend at work said she thought conflict was Satan's doing and it happened at the "fall" when Adam and Eve sinned and were thrown out of the Garden of Eden. She believed before that time they got along perfectly, for that was God's plan. It's an interesting concept, and probably true.

Rebuilding Jim's trust in me was important. I understood his reservation about ever trusting me again. He felt betrayed. But once he began to understand the depth of my shame and realized that I couldn't talk about the incest any sooner, he allowed himself to begin to trust again.

When Jim and I were first married, we took advantage of New Year's resolutions to make them benefit our marriage. We each would come up with *one* thing that we wanted our mate to do that coming year that would enhance our life together. For instance, that first year Jim wanted me to bake a pie every week, while I wanted him to pick up his pants that were left everywhere. The next year, it was important to me that he would never correct me in public, and Jim's request was for me to be more punctual. As each year rolled around, we knew we could ask each other to make a change that would continue throughout our marriage. That little exercise gave us encouragement that the next year would be even better than the last. After seven years of doing this actively, we couldn't think of any more things we needed to ask each other, so we gave it a rest. In our twelfth, eighteenth, and twenty-fifth years of marriage, we needed to address more issues and started using the same exercise. Things have settled down again; however, every New Year's Eve we have the opportunity to ask that same question of each other. Our marriage has been enriched by the yearly New Year's resolutions, which we give to each other.

In December of 1992, Jim and I decided to celebrate our new life together by taking a second honeymoon. After twenty-five years of marriage, we felt like newlyweds. Our daughter Joanna, who was working for an airline, arranged for a wonderful trip to Hawaii. I couldn't imagine a better time.

It pains me to hear people say that victims of sexual abuse are wrecked for life. They can be, but it doesn't have to be that way. Whenever you hear that statement, I hope you will speak up and say, " It doesn't have to be that way," and then hand them this book. Hopefully, this will give them hope for a better life and encourage them to begin their journey to freedom.

Jim and Shirley's wedding day.

8

*There is untapped strength in each of us.
When we face our fears we experience that
wonder.*

I find family interactions very interesting, and that's especially true with my husband's family. When we were dating, it was easy to note the contrasts between my husband's home environment and my own. Jim came from a small, tightly knit family, where the children were at the core of family activities. His parents were people of integrity with an equally high work ethic. Edward and Marie were lifelong residents of Allegan County, Michigan. Together, they raised two children while running a successful vegetable farm on Marsh Road in Plainwell. The rich, black marshland was known for producing some of the most lush and delicious vegetables in the country, and my father-in-law took great pride in making his crops some of the best.

Some of Jim's best memories are waking from a nap on the front seat of his father's International truck, or riding with his father on their Silver King tractor as they plowed and cultivated the fields. Jim considers himself fortunate to have spent countless hours in the shadow of his wise, giant-hearted father. The wonderful memories of working on the farm, hunting, and fishing, as well as the exciting card games, made their relationship a truly remarkable one. His father's influence left lasting imprints upon his children.

Jim's favorite playmate growing up was his vivacious sister Patricia, who was four years older. To hear them reminisce about their childhood pranks makes us all laugh. They have a special brother/sister bond that continues to this day.

Hard work was a way of life for Jim's family, yet recreation was also important. Their upbringing allowed Jim and Patricia to develop a positive attitude toward themselves, life, and work that has served them well.

In my teens, I promised myself that I would never settle for anything less than a wonderful life filled with substance. That didn't mean having wealth, designer clothes, or fancy cars; in fact, those material possessions have meant very little. I prefer shopping at resale shops or garage sales. I was looking for happiness with someone who was rich in the heart with solid moral attributes. I dated a few young men whose primary goal was to get rich, and fast. They would pick me up in their fancy sports cars. One afternoon, when my friend Jeff picked me up, he insisted I drive his shiny red 1963 Corvette convertible. We would go for rides through the wealthy areas of Kalamazoo looking at all the luxurious homes. He would brag how he was going to own one of those mansions one day soon. That was his primary focus. Our relationship didn't last long. To him, I was just a pretty object to parade around. That wasn't substance to me. My goal was to be in a life-long relationship with a man who was far from my example at home. I was determined I would be treated with respect, loved for myself, not my body, given the freedom to air concerns and make decisions—all with a man who would be faithful for life. That is probably every girl's dream, but I knew that man was out there somewhere waiting for me, and I was determined to find him.

I have been told many times that it's very common for victims of abuse to end up in a relationship with someone similar to their abuser. Fortunately, that didn't happen to me, and some say I was just lucky in that respect. I carefully observed everyone whom I dated and compared them to my father. If they had any similar traits, I would not date them a second time. Then, happily, Jim came into my life.

Jim and I had a history together long before there was any serious involvement. I first became aware of Jim in the fall of 1958 while we were in junior high school. I was thirteen, and Jim, fourteen. He hardly knew I existed. I was just another tall, thin gal in the maze of 300 students. Jim was in the class ahead of me, and known by everyone because of his athletic abilities. He loved sports and participated in most of the events. Also, he was hard to miss because he stood a foot above the rest of the boys. I had many chances to observe Jim years before we ever started dating. His pleasant attitude, confidence, and respect for everyone, especially women, are what attracted me to him. Besides all that, he was tall, blond, and handsome.

The following five years of our relationship were rather uneventful. Jim was preoccupied with his sports and many guy friends, and occasionally girlfriends. I was living a complicated double life, a victim of sexual abuse by night and a busy schoolgirl by day. At school, I kept looking for Jim in the halls hoping to catch his eye, but that seldom happened, but during his senior year things started to change. Occasionally, he would throw me a smile or wink while he whizzed around the halls. I thought it was probably because I was a varsity cheerleader. I particularly enjoyed cheering for him, "Petersen, Petersen, he's our man. If he can't do it, nobody can!" My eyes stayed glued on him (like a lot of other gal's) while he was on the field or floor, whichever was the case. However, another cheerleader, who had previously dated Jim, said they were going to get married after they finished college, so I considered him somewhat off limits.

Actually, Jim and I had only two dates while Jim was in high school, and those were late in his senior year. One of the dates was to his senior prom. That date was such an awesome, unforgettable experience. For those of you who believe in love at first date, that's what it was for me. I fell in love at the Senior Prom, and I fell hard. Even though Jim admitted to having a fantastic time, his reaction to our special date was not quite as earthshaking. His focus was getting to and through college. He was looking forward to becoming a teacher and coach; consequently, he couldn't allow himself to get bitten by the love bug, at least not yet. Because there were no further dates, our intense relationship seemed to stop as abruptly as it started.

During Jim's first year at college, he'd occasionally come home to catch a football game. Because I was a cheerleader, out in front, it was easy to spot him. After one exciting evening of high school football (we were playing Otsego, our rival town), Jim came up to me and asked me out on a date. I was ecstatic. I had thought I was out of his life forever. I remember having to break another date so I could go out with him. Once we started dating, we knew we were in a serious relationship that could last a lifetime. Our love and commitment to each other solidified while Jim continued in college. Meanwhile, I finished high school and went on to study nursing. We could hardly stand to be apart.

In August of 1964, Jim asked me to marry him. That was an incredible happy moment. After an evening of Chinese dining in Kalamazoo, Jim leisurely drove me home. While we were sitting on the couch in my parent's living room, Jim threw a pillow on the floor and then got down on one knee. He took my hand, looked me in the eye, and said, "Shirley, I love you so very much, and I want to spend the rest of my life with you. It would make me very happy if you would be my wife. Will you marry me?" I immediately embraced him and said, "Yes. Yes, I'd love to be your wife. I love you so much, too." Then Jim reached in his pocket and pulled out a beautiful half-carat diamond ring and slipped it on my finger. We kissed and embraced in silence, as tears of happiness trickled down our cheeks. Our joy was so intense, I thought the whole world would vibrate with our happiness.

The following June 11, 1965, we were married, and in August we moved into married housing at WMU. September of that same year, I graduated from the Kalamazoo Community College practical nursing school. After graduation, I began working at a long-term nursing facility in Kalamazoo while Jim continued his education. My dream was eventually to go back to college someday and become an art teacher.

Whenever we were around my parents, I continued to put on the great father and daughter image. One way I did that was to worship at my father's church. Part of me was living in denial at that time, and the other was putting up a good front so no one would suspect anything was ever wrong. My pretence sure fooled many, including Jim.

Jim graduated in the summer of 1967 from Western Michigan University with a teaching degree and immediately accepted a teaching position in Mesick, Michigan, a small northern village. There he also coached high school football and, on occasion, drove the school bus. You did many things to support yourself back then, for the salary of a teacher was far from what it is today. I, too, was offered a job at the school as a teacher's aide, which I took because there were no jobs available for nurses in the tiny community.

Now married, every day seemed brighter than the last as I bathed in Jim's love. I savored our time together, for I knew I had a special man to share the rest of my life with. However, I quickly learned that married life was nothing like dating. It seemed I had to fight to spend any time with Jim. After a busy day of teaching, there was coaching football or intramural games for him to supervise. On the weekends, we were busy going to high school games. Jim would ride on the bus with the team and I in the car with friends. In between times, Jim would head for the streams to fish or to the hills to hunt. I missed our time together very much. Being the compliant wife, I never said much about his absence until our sixth year of marriage. When I confessed that other men where looking good to me because I never saw him, he immediately changed so we saw more of each other. He wondered why I didn't say something earlier. Because of my example, I had stayed silent. My mother never complained in her marriage, and she had to deal with a lot worse things than I, so I just kept quiet.

My love for Jim continued to grow, and I wanted to be the best wife I knew how. Subconsciously, I wondered if he would ever start treating me like my father treated my mother, but it didn't happen. I soon learned to relax and enjoy the freedom, privacy, and respect that Jim freely gave me.

When we moved north, the big question then was: what church would we attend, if we were going to go to church at all? At that point in my life, I could have easily given up on all church affiliations. I felt let down by God for not answering my prayers and stopping the sexual abuse in my youth. Doubts about God overcame my desire to go to church. However, I knew if I said I didn't want to go to church, Jim would ask me, "Why not?"—and I was years away from telling him the real reason.

We visited a few churches of the same denomination I grew up in, but they held too many haunting memories. I kept hearing the echo of my father's voice in the pulpit. It seemed all those ministers preached the same sermon, with the same tone of voice and authority. I felt trapped just sitting in front of them. I wanted to get up and preach myself and say, "Be aware of the deceit and piety that hides behind the pulpit. And never assume your children are safe, just because one is a member of the clergy." My experience with my father made me judgmental and suspicious of all clergymen.

A country United Methodist Church and parsonage sat just across the street from the tiny brown bungalow we rented in Mesick. The pastor of the church was one of our first visitors and kindly invited us to his church. To be polite, we thought we would go visit one time, but that one time turned into seven years. That humble church was where my wavering faith began to grow. Their worship service was different from anything I had experienced before. Nothing in it reminded me of my past worship experiences or my father. The music and hymnals were different, as was the style of worship and preaching. They even had two pulpits, one on each side. Later I learned one was called a lectern. Their whole emphasis was on showing God's love to others. As I saw the authentic faith of those dear church folks, I began to grasp a better knowledge of the God they worshiped. And I began to imagine, *maybe there is something to this religion.* At that little church, I realized just how far removed my father was from understanding the truth about God, the Bible, and living the *true* Christian faith. It was under the influence of those ministers and that loving congregation that I began to come to terms with my feelings about my father. I realized it was time for me do something about my hate for him, but accomplishing that goal seemed impossible. Besides, he deserved it. I stalled even longer until I learned how repentance and forgiveness worked.

My legalistic religious upbringing reinforced that if you didn't forgive those who sinned against you, you were sinning. And because I was never taught what real forgiveness was and how it worked, I new I could not be a Christian for it was impossible for me to forgive the sins of my father.

On my spiritual journey I finally found the truth about forgiveness which made it possible to remain a Christian and forgive my father. What I learned is, forgiveness does not make the offence any less nor dismiss the huge impact it has had upon my life. Forgiveness does not say it is "OK and everything is hunky dory". Forgiveness does not always mean reconciliation. Forgiveness does not mean my feelings don't matter and that I can't talk about the abuse. Forgiveness does not mean I cannot confront my abuser or receive the help I need to move forward. Forgiveness does not mean you forget the abuse ever happened. Don't I wish it did!

Forgiveness means I give the situation to God and allow him to deal with those who abused me or abandoned me. It allows God to be the judge and execute his judgment. It means I don't have to hold on to the hate, pain or grudges anymore for I know God will make things right.

Forgiveness allowed me to *let go* so I could have energy to heal and move on. I selfishly forgave for my benefit. I was not doing my father a favor and I was not a saint. I was desperate and determined to not allow my past to ruin my life any further. I believe that by allowing forgiveness to enter the picture I was free to heal. The second reason I forgave was to obey God. I needed to surrender to God's ways and let him be in charge of my healing, and God's ways include forgiving. I admit that forgiving was the last thing I wanted to do. I resisted it for over 30 years. I don't think we ever want to forgive, but for those who do healing happens.

In my search for Scriptural truth I found there are two times we need to forgive. The first is when the deed is done, and the second is when the abuser asks for forgiveness. I found that God does not give us the gift of forgiveness until the sinner asks for forgiveness and changes. (Change is proof of repentance). Jesus paid the price and shed his blood for our sins. He forgave us on the cross and is waiting for us to come to him and receive his gift of forgiveness for ourselves. When we come he gives it freely. Then Jesus says, "You are forgiven. Go and sin no more."

As a Christian, Jesus is my example and I need to forgive those who sin against me. Then once the one who has harmed me asks for my forgiveness and repents I need to tell them I forgive them. We are not obligated to tell them we forgive them until they ask, even though we have forgiven them in our heart.

One gal told me she had forgiven her rapist and was wondering when she should tell him. She felt guilty as a Christian for not telling him she forgave him. I asked her if he had asked for forgiveness and she said "no". She said he had not admitted to the rape yet. My advice was to wait for his admission and repentance before she gave him her gift of forgiveness. She could put herself in danger if she went to him any earlier. God knows our true heart and we do not have to feel guilty for not telling a non repentant soul "I forgive you". What we are told to do is to forgive and pray for those who abuse and hurt us. They certainly need prayer. I prayed for my father that someone would come and help him so he would not hurt anyone else.

Our abuse can make us into undesirable people if we do not forgive and let it go. Otherwise, we can become consumed with hate for that person and that hate radiates through us even though we do not realize it. Unforgiveness causes a host of negative personality and physical traits. And those traits can alienate us from those we love and care about. Forgiving your abuser is a gift you give yourself. It frees you to become the person you were created to be. It allows the memory of the abuse to stop hurting you.

Forgiving does not mean the deed did not matter, or it was not important for both are lies. It did matter and was very hurtful and important. Forgiveness validates the actions happened and then puts the punishment and future of the abuser in God's hand, allowing God to judge and sentence. We no longer have to carry the vendetta for our abuser. We are free!

God tells us to give him our burdens, and hate and vengeance are heavy burdens to carry. We need to release them and give them to their rightful owner. Let them go and give them to God. Refuse to spend your time and energy on such thoughts. We need to work on healing not hating, if we don't we are doomed to a life of despair, ill health and loneliness.

When my father finally told me he was sorry and repented, I told him "I forgive you." He was very thankful and began to weep. From that time on, his greatest struggle was forgiving himself. I doubt he ever did, but because he repented and confessed his sins not only to me but also to God, he died a forgiven man.

Forgiveness is a gift to the one who offended us, as Jesus' gift of forgiveness is to us for our sins. Forgiveness does not dissolve the legal ramifications for crimes. There are consequences for breaking the law and sexual abuse is against the law. When you have forgiven your offended, you will find it easier to move forward past your abuse and experience a new life.

I thought forgiving my father was an impossible task until I gave God permission to work that miracle in my life. The first hurdle I needed to get over was, wanting to forgive him. I did not feel he deserved my forgiveness.

Moving forward requires us to make new habits and to get rid of old hurtful ones. Every time painful memories came into my mind, I had to refuse to go there. I would tell myself, "Let it go! Forgive!" This had to become a habit. Although it was not easy, it was necessary so I could exchange those moments of hate for a lifetime of health and happiness. It was a choice of what was more important to me: peace of mind and my health, or to dwell on my abuse and hate my father? I don't think I could have done this without Gods help. I had such animosity towards my father.

As a diversion from the memories of the incest, I would go sit at my piano and plunk away. Soon, I realized I was not just plunking anymore but creating new tunes, and they were soothing and comforting. I started writing songs about God's beautiful creations, and all the good things in my life. Slowly, I began to think of the abuse less and less, and consequently my hate for my father also began to lessen. At the same time, a new awareness of God began to evolve. I want to clarify that I still feared my father and thought he was crazy. For those reasons, I kept my distance from him, as I should have. My father was a sex offender and not to be trusted. Incest is a serious crime.

I have since realized what an important gift I was given in my ability to play the piano and compose music. It became my sanity; a wonderful medium that helped me to refocus. Something beautiful replaced my ugly thoughts, and every time I play my music, I am reminded of that wonderful exchange.

As I began to release my hate and forgive my father, the rippling effects from the abuse, such as fear, hate, intimidation, self-condemnation, vulnerability, lack of self-confidence, feelings of inadequacy, and the destructive "need to please everybody", also began to go away. That step of mercy toward my father began a real change in my heart. Forgiveness didn't happen overnight. It took a while, but it happened, and it was complete. I believe I experienced a miracle, and that supernatural experience set me free from the incest experience.

As my healing process continued, I began to pity my father. At one time, I thought of myself as a shameful, weak, and flawed individual because of the way my father treated me. But now it was just the reverse. I saw my father as the shameful, weak, and needy one. This new insight also helped to retrieve my self-worth. My father was a mess, worse than I.

Having the influence of sincere ministers at that crucial time in my life also helped to restore my faith in the clergy. I realize it is a very small percent of clergy who commit sexual sins against their children or parishioners, yet it was natural for me to be suspicious of them all after what my father had done to me.

I've learned that no matter who our spiritual leader is, it is just good common sense to ask questions, and get to know the men or women who minister to us. Don't assume they are sinless for no one is. I also found it important to study for myself what is true, and not just accept whatever I'm told. I believe it is important to pray for wisdom and guidance not only for ourselves, but also for all who are in positions of authority, including clergy. Divine guidance is extremely important.

Anger was another emotion I had to learn to own. As a child, I was not allowed to show any form of anger. Whenever I experienced something that made me angry, I learned to suppress it. I couldn't even look at my father when he was doing something troubling, for fear of getting punished myself. If I reacted in any way to what was happening, I would get my hair yanked or butt kicked.

I remember one troubling evening when my mother put a dish of food on the table. My father took one look at it and then harped at her for feeding him such *pig slop*. He slid the food across the table and got up, grabbed her by the arm and began to kick her in the butt. I was thirteen at the time and was so furious I wanted to scream, but instead I had to sit motionless, afraid to even breathe. My stomach and head ached. I remember sitting silently, trying hard not to react, but I was sure steam must have been shooting out of my ears; I was so upset. When it was safe to go outside, I would run over to the Sandersons' and started jumping on their large inflated tractor inner tube. Up and down, up and down, the bouncing seemed therapeutic as I tried to bounce my troubles away. Many mornings, I would wake up with terrific headaches. I now can attribute them to the tremendous stress I was under as a child.

The stress from childhood sexual abuse is enormous. The only thing I knew to do with my stress and anger was to stuff it, which caused me to be a sick, depressed, low achieving child. My physical activities in school helped to relieve some of my stress but the rest came out in forms of depression, extreme fatigue and migraine headaches.

For over twenty years, I felt guilty for having any anger at all. Christians aren't supposed to have anger; at least, that is what I was taught in my childhood. I continued to question what to do with it until my sister and brother-in-law gave me a book by Max Lucado, entitled *A Love Worth Giving*. In it, Lucado clarifies that anger in itself is not a bad thing. The emotion is God's idea. His book helped me to understand the root cause of most anger, as well as the danger and complexity of displaced anger. His book also helped me to relieve the guilt I had for having anger toward my father. Having anger toward my father may sound like a normal response to you, but because of my religious teachings, I felt guilty about it. (Crazy, I know!)

I've since learned that anger is a fitting and normal response when evil is committed, and I have given myself permission to be angry whenever evil is done. Anger is an important emotion. When anger is appropriately applied, it can be a great tool to correct a wrong. Sometimes we have to get good and angry before we become motivated to do something about a situation. Anger can be a positive force—one that can empower us to take action against a wrong.

When we suppress anger and avoid confronting wrongs, we are allowing those who are committing evil to continue. We become enablers.

Even though my anger for my father was justified, my fear and conditioning made it impossible for me to confront my father, or even let me vent it appropriately. That same handicap affected me for nearly thirty years.

We should be angry when sins are committed, just show it appropriately. *Sins should never be covered up or tolerated quietly.*

There is a story in the Bible about the moneychangers near the temple who were taking advantage of the people who came there to worship. The merchants were overcharging those who were trying to obey the Jewish laws. Jesus was so upset that he tipped over their tables to stop their stealing. God gets very angry when injustices are placed upon others. He hates evil.

When I went back to study the Bible, I found more information regarding anger. In Ephesians 4:26, it says, "Be angry and do not sin." It means I should be good and angry for what my father did to me, but I shouldn't do anything drastic that would put me in prison for getting revenge. The negative energy from my anger needed to be transferred into productive uses.

One of the ways I did this was (with Jim's help) to confront my father and make him accountable for his actions. I also insisted he get help for his perversions and personal pain.

I also became proactive by speaking against such wrongs in my community and addressing sexual abuse issues in churches. I have put my energy into helping others who have been injured by sexual offenders, offering compassion and sharing the knowledge I have learned through my experience.

I've learned anger is an important, healthy emotion. We are suppose to own it, and when handled properly, a lot of good can come from it.

 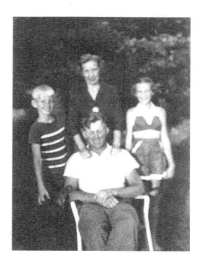

LEFT: Jim and sister, 1948. RIGHT: Jim and family, 1953.

Jim playing basketball.

LEFT: Prom night, 1963.

BELOW: Shirley graduates from nursing school.

ABOVE: Jim and his dad in 1985.
BELOW: Jim and sister.

9
I found a jewel in the shipwreck.

What I am relating to you about my walk of faith
came from years of searching. Because my perpetrator was
also a minister, I had serious questions about my father's
preachings and the God he claimed to know. They were
real questions that needed answers before I could begin to
accept the Christian faith again. Thus, I began an earnest
search for the truth about God (if there was one), and, if
God existed, how he could allow such things as incest to
happen.

During this time, I took a class on the five major
religions in the world: Hindu, Shinto, Islam, Buddhism,
Judaism and compared them to what Christianity had to
offer. I also continued to read what others had to say about
different faiths.

What was particularly alluring about Christianity is
the promise of a wonderful rich afterlife, and it wasn't
contingent upon my good works. Nor did I have to come
back in the next life hoping to do well enough to desire it.
With Christianity, getting into heaven is based only upon
my belief and love for God, and faith in His son Jesus. If I
confess my faith in God and in His son Jesus, I am assured
of going to heaven. This is clarified in the Holy Bible in

Romans chapter 10 verses 9-13, Acts chapter 4 verse 12, and in Matthew 22 verses 37-39.

As I began to study more, I found insight that helped me to conclude that the faith of my youth was worth salvaging. In this chapter, I share how I came to that conclusion, and I hope my findings will add to your understanding as well.

Because this book is written for all people of all faiths and backgrounds, I feel it might be helpful to share what my childhood was like growing up in a Christian family. I think this information will help to enlighten you to the struggles a believer in Christianity can have under my circumstances.

In my childhood, I attended worship services twice on Sunday, plus I went to Sunday school. Wednesday evenings were Bible study and prayer meeting. Thursday nights brought youth meetings with Bible studies. There were also scheduled choir practices every week. On Saturday mornings during my elementary years, I attended protestant catechism. I became well versed in the religious teachings of my conservative Christian denomination. It seemed natural to make the decision to be a follower of Christ and accept God's gift of salvation. My child's mind thought, however, that God could have chosen a better way than the death of His only son to make salvation happen. Death by crucifixion seemed a bit drastic. I was also under the impression that God's love was conditional. I was taught to fear God, and I took it literally, for I saw Him as a man in the sky with an iron rod in his hand, ready to use it if anyone got out of line. Consequently, I approached Him very timidly and would say only prayers that I thought would please Him. The *personal relationship* phrase I heard in church didn't quite make sense, for how could you have a deep relationship with a God you feared? Yet, because of His power, and because I tried to do everything

I could to please Him, I assumed He would always come to my aid, especially when sin was involved.

During the years of my sexual abuse, doubts about God and His omnipresence skyrocketed, and I found myself thinking, "Where is God anyway? Did He really mean it when He said He would always be with me and never forsake me?" I recalled singing church songs that rang, "Only believe, only believe, all things are possible, only believe." Well, I did believe, but I thought, "What good was my believing, if God wouldn't help me with such an important issue as incest? If God really existed, and chose not to answer the prayers of a child in need, whom would He help?" Too many prayers of my youth went unanswered and too many pleas to spare me from my father's evil hands were ignored. Because I felt my prayers were ignored, I stopped praying, and my faith nearly disintegrated altogether. I decided then that if there was a God, He was God of the universe, creator of all things. As for the rest, I was on my own to make it in this life the best I knew how. I think a lot of people today share that same belief.

In my eyes, my father butchered the truth about God and the Bible. It seemed he would preach the Ten Commandments on one day and then break nine of them the next. It was no wonder my faith went caput.

In Stephen Seamand's book *Wounds That Heal*, he claims that our disappointments with God are often the children of false expectations.

Those expectations start with false teachings and indoctrinations. I also believe my abandonment issue with God began when my father abandoned his responsibility as a father. If my father, my religious teacher and mentor, thought I was so insignificant that he could treat me like he did, I only assumed God must think the same about me, for He never came to my rescue. I became convinced that I was definitely not a loved child—by man or God.

Tinker, a good friend of mine, expressed to me that she thought it was remarkable I didn't lose my faith completely. I agreed whole-heartedly with her. I maintain to this day that the near destruction of my belief system was the most serious consequence of my abuse. For in my estimation, if we lose our faith, we have lost the most important thing there is. I explained to Tinker that I came so close to giving it all up, but then asked myself, "What would I gain if I forfeited my belief in God?"

For a short while, I tried to imagine an existence without God. That didn't last long. It was ludicrous for me to even try, for the earth is filled with such beauty, and the heavens with such order and mass, that I couldn't deny there must be someone or something mighty in charge. Besides, life without believing in God seemed empty and meaningless. A life without God also omitted any hope of an afterlife, and that wasn't appealing either. And then, there is always the question, "What if the Bible is true, and there is a God?" At the end of my life, I would be left hanging.

I started admitting I did believe in God, but I had questions and reservations about the Almighty that troubled me, and I certainly didn't think the God I read about in the Bible wanted any kind of a special relationship with me. I recognized then that my decision to abandon my faith would have been made more out of my disappointment with God rather than lack of belief in Him. I decided to keep my faith in God; however, I believed God wasn't someone I could rely on in times of need. After all, He allowed the incest to happen. I expressed those exact thoughts to God. That frank admission was an important beginning to a meaningful faith.

In my search to find out more about the God in the Bible, I found inspiration in books by authors who seemed to understand Him a whole lot better than I, and I came to understand why God allows bad things to happen. As I started to understand why God created us, and the purpose of our lives, my doubts about His devotion and love for His children began to fade.

This new awakening was comforting, and it left me eager to continue my search for more truths about God. Focusing on God and His greatness became another diversion from my childhood nightmares, and His teachings ultimately became the solution for my problems.

As I relate my findings further, I hope you will gain, as I did, an understanding of why God allows such evil to happen.

While reading the Bible, I learned that God gave every human being free will. He made us all free agents. It started with Adam and Eve, for they were given it. I read in the second and third chapters of Genesis that they were tempted by Satan and fell into that temptation. They chose to disobey God's one command and, consequently, were kicked out of the beautiful Garden of Eden. Even God felt the consequences of their sin, for He lost a loving relationship with them. Because God's nature is only pure and good, and can't tolerate sin, He set in order a plan of redemption so a loving relationship could be restored. This was not only for Adam and Eve, but for all of humankind. God loves us so dearly that He executed an unheard-of plan. Part of God would come to earth in the form of a human being. He chose to put his seed in a virgin named Mary. Catholics call this the "Immaculate Conception". God's only son Jesus came to teach us, love us, and to take the punishments for all our sins. His sacrifice would clear our slate, and restore our relationship with God. What makes this personal is we each have to believe in Jesus, repent and accept his grace, and join in God's fellowship.

I read that the payback for what God did for us is *more love*. God wants our love and to have a relationship with us. Then He wants us to love others as well for God knows there is power and healing in love. Love is God's signature card. It's his creation and salvation from the pain in life.

God was aware that with our free will, some would unfortunately choose incest, rape, murder, and other sins. It was a great concern of His from the very beginning, which is why He spoke so many times in the Bible about sin and warned us about its consequences. The biggest One is that it separates us from Him. He also told us that hell is very real, and that He didn't want any of His children to go there. I read that in Matthew 5: 29, 30. (Hell is mentioned over fifty times in the Bible.) What Jesus did for us on the cross was to provide a way so that we would never see hell. His sacrificial death became our pardon—our ticket to spend eternity with God our loving Heavenly Father.

Mel Gibson's movie *The Passion of the Christ* depicts the cruelties Jesus experienced—being abandoned, brutally tortured, and then hung on a rugged Roman cross naked, to die. As gruesome as that true story is, God had an amazing master plan for Jesus' life. Jesus was to redeem the human race. The cost was enormous, for it involved unbelievable agony, shame, rejection, abandonment, and a torturous death. But Jesus went ahead and sacrificed His life for ours out of love and obedience. This was not something he looked forward to, rather, what he needed to do for us. He bled tears of blood knowing how difficult this was going to be. Yet, his love for his Heavenly Father and us overcame his fears. More than anything, Jesus wants to *forgive* and *heal us.* (Luke 4:18)

I learned that God agonizes when He sees how people carelessly abuse their free will and choose evil, and that God grieves deeply with us when we are hurt. I know that I was not the only one who ever felt pain or shame. Jesus experienced unbelievable shame when He was suffering on the cross. In fact, all His sufferings were *far* greater than anything I had ever known. Jesus certainly can relate to any pain we have ever gone through. I realize now that when I cried, Jesus suffered with me. He experienced empathy pains right along with me. He detested the sins committed against me even more than I did. Even though I felt a cloud of sin cover me, I was not a forgotten child. That cloud was my father's doings. And what about my abandonment issue? I read in Matthew chapter 22: 46 that Jesus experienced that as well. Jesus cried, "God, my God, why have you forsaken me?" Wow, I cried that same prayer many times myself. Jesus felt utterly forsaken. God had abandoned His own son. He suffered alone while the sins of the world were upon Him. Then Jesus' death and resurrection completed God's redemptive master plan for the human race. The rest is up to us—to believe or ignore and forgo the privileges of knowing God.

I became aware that God had a master plan for my life as well. I was to have a life filled with peace in spite of the evil that was done to me. God was waiting for me to search Him out so He could help me, but it had to be my choice. There is that free will again, and this time it was up to me. It was my choice to come to God and receive His love and instruction or to remain in my miserable state. I am convinced that it was my turning back to God, the surrendering of my will to God's ways, that began the miracle of healing in my heart.

My father abused his free will and chose to sin and drag me into it with him, despite the fact that he knew better. To make things worse, he chose not to turn from his sins, but rather to continue in them for years. I remember begging my father to stop and to get help. There was help available for him, but it had to be his decision to get help. Unfortunately, I was the innocent victim trapped under his control, falling prey to his selfish desires. God allowed my father to sin against me because it was part of the free will He gave to all humankind, *not because I was a child to be ignored or wasted.* God had a plan to turn the evil I experienced into good. He does for everyone who experiences evil.

God desires us to be in continuous fellowship with Him, and that we walk in His light and experience His love. *Within that love, wonderful things can happen. I've learned that lives can be transformed and hearts and bodies can be healed.*

God yearns for us to call Him Father and come to Him with our problems, much like we parents desire our children to come to us. As I gingerly began to put my trust in God, I started to feel a new and genuine connection. I was experiencing the love of my Heavenly Father for the first time. He had been wooing me gently back to Him for some time. God wanted to reach me and teach me. But I had to be willing to connect with Him before I could receive all He had for me – peace, joy and the abundant life.

God has planned for each one of us a fulfilling life. Jesus called it "abundant life". God created us to heal and He urges us to pursue healing. When we avoid overcoming our abuse, we deny ourselves a chance at experiencing the abundant life.

As I put more effort into developing an understanding of God, I began to notice that I was becoming more like the person I wanted to be. My heart was softening. I became more patient. Irritants didn't bother me as much. I started looking at the big picture of life as well, and I found it easier to let things go. I was *beginning* to take on God's nature, and soon I realized I didn't have any animosity for my father anymore. Actually, the words "Help me to forgive my father, Lord," that I uttered a few years earlier became a reality. I didn't hate my father anymore; in fact, I began to see him in the same light God does. *I experienced a healing of the heart.* God's love was rubbing off on me, and it made my spirit glow.

Our grandson Gabriel often comes for a visit and ends up spending the night. One evening, after a day of play and fun activities together, he looked up at me and said, "Grandma, when I grow up, I want to be just like you!" My head must have swollen to the size of the moon with pride. *Wow, what a compliment*, I thought. He loved me so much that he wanted to be just like me. I think that is how it should be with our Heavenly Father, that we love Him so much we want to be just like Him. I believe when we show sacrificial love to another, we are the closest to being like God that we could ever be.

After I found my way back to the faith of my youth, I realized my childhood faith had changed dramatically. I no longer viewed God as a demanding, frightening and authoritarian figure. God had become a vital, constant companion, the perfect loving friend who accepts me as I am, who gives me inspiration to do even better. The one I feared became my comforter and my counselor. The servant Jesus I read about in the Bible became my Savior.

The jewel I found in my shipwreck was a brilliant new faith in God, something I never thought I would experience—and what a priceless find.

10

We carry in our mouth the most important key in the world.

As a victim of incest, I was victimized and wronged in the most personal way possible. And because my father was also my religious mentor, I believe I experienced the ultimate betrayal. The impact of my abuse lingered throughout my adult years. I did not realize how traumatic the effect was on me until I was in my 40s. When I finally acknowledged my problems, I knew I needed to find someone to talk to. My big question was, "Who do I dare go to for help? A family member, a close friend, a professional?" It had to be someone whom I trusted, one who would keep what I said in confidence. But before all this could happen, I still had to overcome what my father had told me so many times before: "No one would ever believe you. I'm a very respected man." My shame and childhood fears regarding my father were still very much alive, which made it nearly impossible to tell anyone.

Ever since my early twenties, I had been writing down my thoughts and poems in a tablet. Later, I learned I was journaling. I found writing to be therapeutic. At least

I was doing something about my circumstance, even if it was only on paper. I had a secret desire that someone, some day, would find my writings and figure out what my hidden sorrow was. Then I wouldn't have to talk about it. Well, no one ever found my writings; however, they have been helpful, especially when I went back to write this book. My writings helped me to recall certain events, but, more importantly, they were a good reminder for me to see how far I had come on my journey to wholeness.

In the summer of 1991, I finally found my *safe* person to talk to. It was my youngest sister, Ginger. Her words in a family conversation ignited my courage and started me talking about the incest.

Jim and I and our three daughters had been camping with my sisters and brothers that summer. We were in my sister Georgia's pop-up trailer eating breakfast one morning when the subject of our father came up. My oldest sister Naomi exclaimed that she was always jealous of me while we were growing up because of all the attention our father gave to me. She was convinced I was his favorite. As those words rolled off her tongue, I began to simmer.

Then my sister Ginger abruptly broke into the conversation by saying that she didn't think I was his favorite at all. She proceeded to tell the events she remembered as a young girl. She said our father would often come into our bedroom in the middle of the night and bother Shirley. She said she heard us whisper and have bad arguments between us. As soon as she spoke, my heart screamed, "Yes!" Now I knew of someone who would believe my story. Ginger could prove that my father came into our room at night. Even though she was only in her pre-teens at the time, and didn't know exactly what had transpired, she knew something bad had happened. My father's words, "No one would ever believe you." began to evaporate. Ginger's revelation was monumental.

A few weeks later, Ginger and her family came to visit us on the lake for a mini-vacation. That provided the perfect opportunity for me to tell her the whole story. Ginger was also a family therapist. What an added bonus! With her listening skills and insight, Ginger gave me the comfort and support I needed. With tears in her eyes, she embraced me and said, "Oh, my, yes! That's what father was doing to you! I can't believe I never figured that out myself." She continued, "Shirley, I'm so glad you finally told me. I can't believe you've held this in for all these years. No wonder you've been so sick. Shirley, Jim needs to be told. You must tell him."

My first reaction was, "No! No, at least not yet!" But her words cut to the truth, and I knew she was right. I had withheld my story already too long. It was time for me to share my deepest pain with my husband. That following Sunday after we took our girls to camp, the dreaded conversation finally began.

To have a good friend with whom you can bare your soul is one of the greatest gifts on earth. I'm talking about one who will listen; I mean *really* listen, to what you have to say, even when you're repeating yourself over and over again. I'm talking about a friend who will put you first and go the distance no matter what it takes to help you. That is a rare person.

My husband became that kind of friend to me, and he proved it over and over, especially in those months following the time I came out with my story in 1991. Through him, I experienced a depth of love I never knew existed.

I consider myself fortunate to have had the love and support from my family and friends. I also had a compassionate counselor who educated me and consoled me, but my husband became my *live-in* therapist. He also was my advocate and bore most of the burden of caring for me.

Jim was on duty 24/7 in spite of the fact that he had his own personal issues regarding my father and the incest. He demonstrated sacrificial love, time and time again, as I would pour out my heart to him. I was so relieved that I could finally talk about the incest that my words flowed out of me like Niagara Falls. He'd listen to me for hours, then he would have to get up and go to work the next day. My brother David, a social worker/family counselor, reminded me that most husbands couldn't do that because it is too emotionally and physically exhausting. They have to rely on a therapist to care for the emotional health of their loved one. Jim is an unusual man. I knew that before I married him.

One fall evening in 1992, I was still baring my soul to Jim. With his soft hairy arms cuddled around me, he listened again to what I needed to say. I must have rattled on for an hour or so before I stopped. When he said to me, " Shirl, is there anything else you need to say about this? If so, I'm listening," I stayed quiet. "Or," he continued, "is it time to give it a rest and put it behind you?" I was startled by his remark. Yet his words were like a light popping on in my head. *Hmm, maybe my talking about it had run its course.* It had monopolized so much of my time and energy, and was the subject of our conversation nearly every night. *I realized then that it was time for me to move on.* Jim's remark became a turning point. Yes, we still talk about incest issues as they arise, and any time I feel the need, but the topic is now always in the past tense and that's a very good place for it.

Once we have shared our hurt and nursed our emotional wounds, there comes a time when we must move forward and put the past in its proper place. When we don't, we allow the past to control us and destroy any hope of recovering. We can replay the sad events of our lives over and over again until that same depressing story begins to dominate us and our lives become unlivable.

The purpose of sharing our hurt with another is not to keep us a prisoner to it, but rather to free us from the pain it has brought us. If we stay in a negative, repetitive pattern of thinking, we allow our perpetrator to continue to abuse us. This is why we need to learn to develop a new life away from our abusive experience and let go of the painful memories. That requires a vigilant effort on our part. New habits need to be established so we don't slide back into old thought patterns. Developing a new interest or hobby or taking a class can help to facilitate this. For me, playing the piano and composing music became a wonderful diversion. Whenever I would find myself regurgitating past hurts, I would stop myself and make a beeline for the piano.

As I journeyed toward health, I realized how important it was for me to wean myself from those I had grown emotionally dependent upon. I needed to brave it on my own. Like walking on a mended leg after the cast has been taken off, I needed to learn to walk alone and become strong and independent. This was a real growing time in my life. As I tested the waters alone, my self-confidence grew, and I found I wasn't a simple girl like my father had said. It felt good to be able to handle life's situations by myself, and to have assurance in my own judgments. I was beginning to establish my own identity and boundaries, and I was becoming proud of who I was. My once strained face was beginning to show signs of life and genuine joy.

I knew of a woman who loved the support she received so much that she never wanted to move on. She enjoyed all the attention. Ten years later, she was still going to counselors and talking about her tragedy. Sadly, she wore out all of her friends, family, and many counselors in the first five years. Her life was a pitiful repeat of the tragedy she had already lived through. Her rut was so deep that even medication had little effect. She never connected with the next step, *nor wanted to*. Her abuse became her identity. What a sad way to live, and what a pitiful waste of time and energy!

Life is not fair, and some of us learn that early in life. Our biggest challenge is to not allow our hardship to cripple us for the rest of our lives. Life is full of bittersweet, and the sooner we stop our "poor me" attitude, the sooner we will taste the *sweet* part in life.

I never bought into the concept that the world owes us special privileges because of our misfortune. My sister-in-law Patricia has helped me avoid that trap, and has taught me much about being a wounded survivor. Even though her experiences are not related to sexual abuse, her pain and loss are enormous.

After years of struggling, her oldest son died of cancer. He was only fourteen. Then a few years later, she nearly died from a misdiagnosed health condition, which left her with a chronic, disabling condition—lymphedema. However, you will never hear her complain or dwell on her adversities. No, quite the contrary. With the knowledge she's gained, she started a support group to help others. She has suffered more than most, yet she has learned to make lemonade out life's bitter lemons. She refuses to let her tragedies destroy her life or those around her, and in the process, she's become a lighthouse of inspiration for others.

Our tragedies can become the golden threads in life that makes us shine as we learn and grow from our experiences. There are many who have been hurt deeply from a variety of sources, and those who let go of their "victim thinking" are those who move forward and find happiness. It is our own responsibility to pursue health and to find joy in life.

One young woman who was brutally beaten and raped said, "My body was used by an evil man for two hours. I am not going to give him another minute of my life by sulking around and feeling sorry for what happened to me. I have a life to live!"

What an attitude! She realized she wasn't wrecked. She was just horribly wronged.

Victim thinking inhibits our recovery. It stunts our growth. Besides that, who wants to be around those who pout or act like the world owes them? Whenever I feel a pity party coming on, I refuse to go there, for I know it will only delay my happiness.

During the course of my healing, I've found meditation and prayer to be very beneficial. As I would express my disappointments, disillusionments, and pain to God, I would be reminded to count my blessings, look for all the good in life, and to pray for others. During my low times, I would focus on others who were hurting and do good deeds for them, and it works. Focusing on others revives the spirit. It's the greatest pick-me-up I know.

I heard a speaker once say that after we have told our story we are to be mentors, to help others through their time of crisis. Her words reminded me of the importance of being more than just a survivor. Through experiencing all the TLC others gave me, I realized how essential it is to be an example of hope for another. We need to share our stories. Telling is not only transforming for the teller, it can also be beneficial for those who hear it.

I love the simple things in life, such as having a good laugh and a hot cup of tea while chatting with a dear friend. During one of those enjoyable times, my friend Donna and I were discussing the subject of happiness and what we would have done differently in our lives if we had the chance. It wasn't hard for me to be the first to jump in. There is no doubt that the first thing I would have done differently would have been to break the silence about the incest earlier in my life. Opening up is the critical first step toward eliminating a bitter chapter in one's past, and the sooner we do, the better off we will be.

In the book *The Sacred Romance,* Brent Curtis and John Eldredge compare the pain that is inflicted upon us to arrows that are driven into our hearts. We each need someone who can help pull those arrows out so our wounds can heal. Jim's words of encouragement and gentle hands not only pulled the arrows out, but also became the balm that started the healing process in my heart.

For those who do not have a significant person to pull out those arrows of sorrow, family members, friends, counselors, members of support groups, rabbis, ministers, and priests can help. It is important that we find someone and allow that person to help us so we can heal.

Jim, on occasion, has affectionately called me an "angel". I respond by saying, "If I ever am one, it is because of you, for you are the one who gave me my wings." I truly believe that.

In spite of my past, my life has been far from a lost cause. I have wonderful memories of Jim and my children, even in our early years together. They are tucked in my heart forever and *outshine* my abusive past. I have often told Jim that my life started the day I married him, and that our life together has made up many times for those horrible years in my youth. Without Jim, however, I've often wondered where I would be today.

Through the years Jim continues to be my sounding board, as I am for him. He is a solid arm to lean on, and a prayer I repeat often is, "Thank you, Dear God, for giving me such a marvelous husband. He is such an awesome person to spend my life with. I am so blessed."

While I am finishing this book, I am also attending to my husband's physical needs. It's now my turn to take care of him, and I love it. My once healthy, strapping husband, for the first time, is experiencing the woes of being seriously ill. He is recovering from a ruptured bowel. I've enjoyed being his private duty nurse and having him lean on me for a change. I am thankful I'm *healthy* and able to care for him. I could not have done this if I had not begun my journey to health.

It also feels good to be whole enough to focus on the emotional needs of my family, especially my husbands.

When my story first came out Jim put his needs and concerns regarding my abuse on the back burner so he could focus on me and my needs. It was now time for me to focus on him and help him work thru his personal issues. It was also time to concentrate on reestablishing his faith and trust in me. Even though intellectually Jim understood why I kept the secret, he still took a big arrow to the heart and I needed to help that wound heal.

Jim's grief was deep for many reasons. He hurt for me and for all the pain I experienced in my childhood. He hurt because I did not tell him about the abuse sooner. He anguished over my father and his evil deeds. He hurt for our family as he realized how the rippling affects from my abuse contributed to our family's problems. He grieved for the years of lost intimacy, and for not picking up on the signs of my sexual abuse.

As I encouraged Jim to talk about his concerns he began to open up and spoke from his heart. It was then I realized the depth of his pain. I also realized I had an important role; to help him heal. He needed my ears, my understanding, and he needed me to meet his needs. Even now, occasionally, he will mention a concern that pertained to my abuse and we will talk it through.

Jim understands only too well, the challenges spouses face when married to a victim of sexual abuse, and he makes himself available to talk with any spouse about sexual abuse issues.

I have heard Jim say many times: "Life isn't fair; Things aren't always as they seem; and you can't change the past." He also has been quoted as saying, "There are situations in life that we have no control over. During those times we need to rely on our faith to help us move forward."

Jim's practical philosophy has helped him through out life, and is one we could also benefit from adopting.

When Jim and I are invited to speak to groups about our story, you will often find a huddle of men around Jim asking personal questions that only he can answer.

Through exposing my story and learning to overcome my sexual abuse, our relationship has grown tremendously. We've learned that sexual abuse does not have to dampen or destroy a marriage, and we hope our story will help other couples experience the same growth, healing and intimacy.

Jim and Shirley, 2004.

11

Could emotional pain be the ultimate truth serum?

Earlier I mentioned that I insisted my father get into serious counseling. I also had an opportunity to go to counseling with my father and mother. While talking with my father and our family counselor, I learned a great deal about my father, Martin Lillie. For nearly seventy years, he had carried around a huge backpack of pain, shame, and anger. Much of it was from his tragic childhood and from the things he had done to try to remedy his pain. It was disheartening to learn how badly my father's dad had physically and emotionally abused him. To alleviate his pain, my father would walk the village streets looking for love and acceptance, but instead would land in the hands of merchants who used him for their own sexual gratification. He also shared how he found himself in similar circumstances when he was sent away to boarding schools.

I truly felt my father's pain and understood his shame, because I also knew the sting of being unloved and abused by a father. Yet to me, all of the abuse he encountered as a child didn't take him off the hook for sexually abusing me. You would think that sexual abuse would be the last thing he would ever do to his own, for he knew the hurt it brought. I know a lot of people who have been sexually abused, including me, who did not repeat those acts on their children.

Because incest is such a bizarre behavior, the nurse in me can't help but wonder if it is accentuated by a hormonal or chemical imbalance. I will have to wait for the researchers to find that answer.

I realize my father's cruel behaviors were a direct result of the deep hidden pain from his childhood. It was his way of getting back. Overpowering others was a way he tried to cure his lack of self-worth and alleviate his pain. A counselor explained to me that my father's behavior was from the enormous amount of physical and emotional abuse he experienced as a boy, mainly from his father. Our body protects us from additional pain by making us emotionally numb. When that happens, we also become numb to the pain of others, which is why it becomes easy to abuse another. We can't relate to another's pain. A natural response to emotional pain is revenge, which commonly turns into abusive behaviors.

If we don't have the love and support we need and the tools to alleviate our emotional pain, we act out our pain in many different ways, and most often on those closest to us. This was certainly true with my father, for those under his control often felt his wrath. As I began to understand this concept, I realized how the incest happened, as unfortunate as it was. My father abused me because he had no feelings of love for me. That is something no child wants to hear. In a conversation, he confessed that he did not love me, or any of his children. In fact, he told me he had never wanted children, only sex. He explained that he was emotionally numb inside and incapable of loving. He admitted that he even doubted God's love and grace for himself. As I began to understand the *whys* of my abuse, my heart began to soften toward him. I realized how emotionally crippled he was and how devastating the effects of his abusive childhood had been.

A friend once said to me, "I'm not minimizing what was done to you, Shirley, but I think your father's abuse was probably so much worse and his wounds so much deeper. That is why he did what he did." She went on to say his type of abuse is often called toxic abuse. Such terrible abuse often drives victims to be self-destructive, to where they don't value their lives or the lives of others.

During the years of sexual abuse, I would try to minimize what my father had done to me. I would lie to myself and make excuses for him. For a time, I believed the lies he told me, like the one that I was the cause of his sexual desires. Blaming myself was somehow easier than admitting it was my father's lack of love that caused him to do such evil deeds to me. I couldn't allow myself to admit that I was an unloved child, used only for his pleasure. That truth would have been too devastating. My mother's words also didn't help. After she was told about the incest in 1991, she told me that this often happens in families, so there was no need to make a big deal about it. My husband was furious with her remarks and reinforced my claim that incest is a terribly serious crime, against the laws of society and nature—obviously a much larger ordeal than she tried to make it out to be. Her blunt remark made me question her if she had been sexually abused when she was young. She told me she was not.

Dr. Pluger, a family counselor who specializes in sexual abuse, offered my father and me special counsel. I knew my father especially needed it. As my father and I talked to the counselor, I felt a sense of relief come over my father. I believe in my heart that he was glad to be getting some emotional help for his perverted behaviors, even if it was forced upon him. Someone, for the first time, was tending to his deep, infected, emotional wounds. Now my father had begun his own journey to wholeness.

Dr. Pluger realized the complexities of our family problem. After spending hours with my father, he reinforced the need for continued long-term counseling for him. He also made us aware that pedophiles continue their actions unless they get help, regardless of how old they get, and that this problem does not just go away after talking about it a few times. Dr. Pluger diagnosed my father with multiple psychological conditions, including pedophilia.

Webster's Dictionary describes pedophilia as "Sexual perversion in which children are the preferred sexual object."

My mother took offense when Dr. Pluger diagnosed my father as a pedophile. Her comment was, "No! No! The young girls he had sex with wanted it for the money." Her comment infuriated me. No young girl wants painful intercourse with an older man. If she permits it, it is because she is desperate, with great monetary needs. My father took advantage of those young girls because he was a pedophile. Otherwise, he would have gone to older gals or women who were prostitutes. He said he preferred the young ones. Pedophiles are people with twisted minds who need intense therapy, and there is help available for them. (Family counseling centers can direct you to the best sources.)

In 1980, Jim, our oldest daughter Joanna, and I visited my sister Naomi and her family on an island in the West Indies, where she and her husband were working. My father also was working there developing a Christian Boarding School up in the mountains. He knew we also wanted to visit Haiti, so he offered to be our tour guide to that poverty stricken land. The rough terrain and bleak culture was an education in itself. We were truly in culture shock.

As we drove into the capital of Port-au-Prince, my father's behavior became erratic. He insisted that he needed to see a man about some urgent business in the city, although he had not mentioned this business before. The smell of the Haitian air seemed to have an erotic effect on him. In a conversation with my husband in 1991, when my parents came to our house for *the talk,* my father confessed that he often went there to have sex with the young Haitian girls. Now I know what important business he was attending to that evening many years ago, and it also explained his strange behavior that day.

It may sound strange, but in some ways, the last few years of my parents' life were the best they had ever experienced. Very shameful, yes. But at the same time, my father experienced a sense of freedom and even relief that he had never known before, and my mother a sense of understanding. However, he sadly told me that the loss of respect of his children nearly killed him and was the worse blow he had ever endured. That was the price he paid for his actions. We reap what we sow. In time, all his children learned to forgive him.

Dr. Pluger helped my father embark on a walk that would change his life. Six months later, I heard my father finally say to me, "I am so sorry. I had no idea how badly I hurt you. I didn't know what hurt was until I started feeling some for myself." He wept, for he was beginning to feel the pain I had experienced so many years ago. My father's confession and repentance of his sins was huge, not only for him but also for me. His words were what I needed to complete the forgiveness process towards him. His repentance was a gift to me. So many victims never hear "I'm sorry. Please forgive me." or see repentance.

On my father's journey, he also was beginning to grasp the concept of God's great love for him. He still did not think he was worthy of it, even during his last dying moment, and I believe that is why he struggled at the end.

The Christian faith, which I acclaim, reminds me that God's grace covers all sin. Yes, even incest and pedophilia. When Jesus died on the cross, he paid the price for all our sins. I was reminded of that truth when I read Isaiah chapter 44, verse 22. It says God sweeps away our sins like a cloud. They evaporate like the morning mist, never to be remembered again. *That is the ultimate mercy and pardon.*

Even though I experienced freedom from my incest experience and learned how to forgive, the memory of that incest will always be there. Forgiving does not make our memory go blank. The positive side of remembering my past is that I can help others through their difficult time. I can also bring awareness to this social problem so we can attempt to rid it from our society. That, I believe, is one of my missions in life and why the memory of the abuse is supposed to stay with me.

My mother seriously questioned whether I forgave my father. She told me many times that if I really forgave him, I wouldn't have to talk about it or tell anyone. She thought if I had really forgiven my father, I would just tuck my pain away and forget the abuse ever happened. Oh, if it were only that simple! I tried that approach for over 25 years. What do you do with the horrible shame, ill health, and crippling side effects that accompany the sexual abuse if you can't talk about it?

One of the first questions a renowned cardiologist asks his patients is, "With whom do you share your feelings and problems?" He has found in his twenty years of practicing medicine that it is vital for his patients to have a trusted relative or friend with whom they can share their problems. The success of his treatment for them depends upon it. He has concluded that when his patients hide or avoid their problems, it only compromises their physical healing.

I tried to explain to my mother the importance of sharing my story and pain. I told her I needed to talk about it so I could work through it and learn how to eliminate the negative consequences from the incest. I reminded her that telling my story was not done to destroy my father. I don't think my mother completely understood.

The completion of this book comes nearly ten years after the death of my father, and its purpose is far greater than revealing his sins. That is the least of its intent. If my agenda were to destroy my father, I would have yelled *wolf* to everyone, including the press, when I first came out with my story back in 1991 while he was still alive. Instead, I kept my story discrete and only shared it with family members, a few close friends, and with my therapist.

Some people still question where my father's soul is spending eternal life, especially because he was a minister. They ask, "Was he really sorry for what he did, or was he sorry that he got caught?" I think some of both. Only God can answer that question for sure. However, being the optimist that I am, I believe my father's spirit is in heaven. He had hope in God and asked for forgiveness, and I believe God honored His word. Do I think he deserved heaven? No, but God's grace provides a way for everyone.

I think it's ironic that the daughter my father abused was the one who ultimately rescued him. I became an instrument of God, used to pull my father back to Him. He had strayed for many years. I believe I was supposed to tell my story so my father could be made accountable for his actions and receive help. Most importantly, he needed to experience God's love and forgiveness and find healing for himself.

My father lived long enough on this earth to make peace with God, himself, and with me. He definitely felt the shame and repercussions from his sins. He also received the comfort he desperately needed for his own personal pain. Even greater, he died having hope of eternal life in heaven. At seventy-two, my father passed on to his new home on February 11, 1996, in Fort Lauderdale, Florida. He died from toxic poisoning, a complication from a homeopathic treatment for prostate cancer that he received in Mexico.

Because sex was so important to my father, even at his age, he chose not to have his prostate removed for fear he would become impotent. It seemed sex was more important than life itself.

I am glad I had the opportunity to confront my father about the incest before he died. All the important words that needed to be said between us were said. If we had had more time, I think even more mending would have come. However, I am grateful we had an opportunity to get at the root of what plagued us both. The issue of the incest was definitely on the mend, and we were eager to close that chapter between us.

12
It's truly not over even when you think it is.

I thought that my father's death would bring an end to all of my nightmares for good, but surprisingly, that was not the case. At night, I would now dream that I had also died, and in heaven my father continued to molest me. I would wake up in fright, thinking there was no safe place on earth or in heaven where my father could not take advantage of me. When I would awaken, I would know that the abuse could never happen, but in my dream I would call out to God to help me just like in the past, but He never came. I was reliving in my dreams what my father had done to me in my youth in spite of the fact that he was dead. This was ludicrous, yet terrifying. I remember hating to go to sleep at night for fear those nightmares would recur.

Heaven had always been a wonderful place in my mind. I would daydream of how beautiful and peaceful it must be. It was easy for me to envision how happy my deceased loved ones were up there, and I was looking forward to joining them someday when my time came. But now my father had literally put the fear of death in me. *I found I was afraid to die for the first time in my life.* To some folks, this may seem a bit trivial, but for me it was a big thing. Obviously, the fear of my perpetrator was still there, and stronger than I liked to admit. This fear I also needed to share with my husband. Jim and I continued to talk until this problem was resolved, but it took a few months. I have to admit that heaven is still not the same place I once envisioned. Maybe there is more work that needs to be done.

When I first disclosed the incest, I had an unexplainable problem—that of wanting to protect my father. I experienced the terrible conflict of wanting to tell my story, but also desired to protect him from the consequences. I struggled with that dilemma until I recognized it was primarily fear-related. (I also realized the seriousness of his sins and what repercussions existed for him. Incest is a serious crime).

Even after I came out with my story, I was still very fearful of my father. Writing this book brought a certain amount of anxiety, and my father has been gone for nearly a decade. Our childhood fears stay with us a long, long time, especially if they are associated with shame and pain. However, that anxiety did not stop me from writing. I believe my drive to complete this book came from a divine source with a divine purpose; otherwise, I don't think I would have had the stamina to make this happen. Writing a memoir of this nature is extremely difficult and exhausting.

The shock of our lives came just two months to the day after my father died, when we learned of my mother's sudden death. She was killed April 11,1996, in an automobile/truck accident in Fort Lauderdale, the day after celebrating Easter with my sister Naomi. That was a double tragedy, because we also lost our dear Aunt Rachel, my mother's sister, who was riding with her at the time of the accident. We children felt the wrenching grip of death like never before. We had made plans to develop a closer relationship with our mother now that she was widowed.

While she was living with our father, our time with her had been very limited. His priorities were always other than spending a lot of time with his children, whether we were young or grown. He demanded my mother's constant emotional support, which she dutifully gave him. After years of living with my father's brainwashing, she grew emotionally dependent upon him. She had little knowledge of the world of finance, so after his death, she allowed her children to help her with all her affairs. For fifty-one years, she never knew a life away from my father except for the two brief months right after his death. During that short time, we children were delighted how well she was doing on her own. We saw amazing strength in our mother and were eager to see more growth and learn more about her. Consequently, we felt robbed of the precious time we could have spent with her.

I had resolved my feelings about my mother's lack of protection for me a long time ago. When we were growing up, I witnessed her being treated like one of us children. Back then, I considered her just as powerless as we were. I saw her as a victim of my father's authoritarian hand. She was scolded and lectured on submission for so long, she thought it was a sin not to obey my father, even when he systematically abused his rights as a husband. I witnessed her being emotionally crushed and physically kicked. I was there when my father ordered her up to their bedroom and demanded to have sex, doing so with the door wide open. I related only too well to the pain she was enduring and felt pity for her. I'm sure in her mind, she minimized her abuse and rationalized that it was her duty to tolerate my father, for she was, after all, his wife, and didn't think she had any other options.

What hurt me was the cold shoulder my mother gave me during my teen years. She was especially short, and made me feel like I was a burden to have around. I was always respectful to her, yet she always had her guard up around me as if to say, "Don't talk to me." Her distance puzzled me. Later, I realized that even though she denied knowing about the incest, she resented me for the interest my father had in me and for the conflict I brought into the family. Once I was married and out of the house, my mother's attitude toward me dramatically improved. She was like a new person. Our relationship grew, and I felt loved by her, and we became friends for the first time.

After my father died, my mother mourned his passing. I talked with her every week and she told me that she had a constant pain in her heart. Yet, she was extremely courageous and was looking forward to her new life as a widow and spending time with her children and grandchildren. We each grieved her loss deeply. She survived the best way she knew how and tried to make the best out of every situation. My mother told me that once the children were out of the home, life with my father became more pleasant. She enjoyed the trips they took together even if it was always our father's decision as to where to go and what to do. She found fulfillment in being a tag-a-long and acting as his little servant. While the wife of a president of a Christian boarding school, she enjoyed the opportunities and perks that accompanied that position. My mother loved life, and people young and old alike, and that was evident to all. I realize that as a protector, she failed me in a serious way, and that failure is one she had to reckon with. Parenting comes with great responsibilities, and protecting our children is one that tops the list.

When I learned that I was the only child out of the seven who was not breast-fed, I wondered if she had less of an attachment to me, and that is partly why she could dismiss what went on.

It wasn't until I had children of my own and realized what an important responsibility I was given, that my real disappointment in her surfaced.

My mother spoke of heaven with great expectations and looked forward to singing in the choirs of heaven. One of her favorite hymns was "I Love To Tell The Story". The lyrics continue with, "Twill be my theme in glory, to tell the old, old story of Jesus and His love." I can still hear her unique voice.

My sister-in-law Patricia asked me if I grieved the passing of my parents. I told her I did, but in a different way than those who grieve the passing of a loved one. I grieved for never having had a mother who was strong enough to do what was best for me. I grieved for not having had a good example of how to have a warm, loving relationship with your daughter. I grieved for never having known what it was like to have a father look at me with pure eyes, to have an interest in me other than sexually, or to demonstrate how a good husband or father is supposed to behave. I grieved for the carefree life I missed in my youth, and for not having trustworthy grandparents for my children, ones to share special, happy times or overnight visits. I grieved that my husband never had a father-in-law with whom he could share man-to-man talks or fishing trips. I grieved over the lost years of intimacy with my husband and for the years of not knowing a loving God. I grieved for the wrongs I committed to escape my abuse and for the people I injured. Yes, I have grieved a lot over the passing of my parents, for they have caused me a lot of grief. However, I also recognized that my grieving was important to my healing. My loss was something I needed to recognize, grieve, cry over, and then finally *get over* in order for me to get past my abuse issues, and find peace and wholeness.

I could tell when my grieving time had finally passed, for it was then that I could revisit my childhood and not be plagued with only bad memories or feel sick. I could begin to thank my parents for giving me life, shelter, food, clothing, and most importantly, my brothers and sisters. While growing up, I had a chance to travel, I met wonderful people, and *I found my husband.* They also passed on to me healthy genes and certain attributes that have made my life enjoyable. Yes, I have many things for which to thank my parents, and for those reasons I can honor them.

We can't choose our parents, but we can choose to be better parents ourselves. I believe if we want to be successful at parenting, we need to get healthy first by examining our own dysfunctions and then work at overcoming and correcting them.

Learning to love well and being authentic is an important component in being a good parent.

13

Love each one as if they were the only one.

From the beginning of our marriage, Jim assumed I would take an active role in our relationship by making decisions and by participating in an equal partnership. That was something foreign to me because of the example at home and how I was programmed. I was handicapped in that respect. All I knew was to follow Jim's lead.

Starting at birth, I was reared to be obedient, to do what I was told no matter what, and not to question. You might say I was raised to be mindless. My father told me I was simple, and that I should not think or question anything I was told. Consequently, I never allowed myself the luxury to think about anything more that what was basic to my physical needs. The children in our home were to be seen and not heard, literally. We were hushed and told to be quiet. I felt the painful consequences that came from not doing exactly as ordered, as did my siblings and my mother, so I fell in line easily. This unfortunately left me easy prey for abuse. In my father's mind, I didn't have the right to refuse, or to be heard. I was so programmed that I thought I didn't have a choice, whether it was incest or anything else that went on in our home. That is why I tolerated the sexual abuse as long as I did. *I was trapped by my conditioning, and by my own sheer ignorance.*

To find an equal partnership in a marriage is beautiful. I was first exposed to that concept through a remarkable couple in my youth. Our family was introduced to Michael and Mary Goodman when we moved to Tipton, Michigan, in 1954, and my father became the minister of their church. They were the "salt-of- the-earth" kind of people who always made time to perform acts of kindness for others.

Do you remember that famous artwork by Grant Wood, "The American Gothic"? It is a painting of a farmer standing beside his wife with a pitchfork in his hand in front of their farm. Well, that couple in the painting closely resembled the Goodman's. I often had opportunities to watch them operate their large sheep and chicken farm. Farming was Michael's second job. After early morning chores were done Michael headed off to work at Tecumseh Products, with Mary's carefully packed lunch in hand. After work, he'd come home and start haying or caring for the animals. Mary's work was never done either. She was always busy in her garden, or feeding the chickens and sorting eggs. Yet, for supper, she always made time to make Michael a homemade pie to go with the evening's meal. Their teamwork was mixed with a strong dose of dedication and love for one another and toward their goals as a family.

Their only child Kay and I instantly became best friends. We were both only seven at the time and bonded like sisters—a bond we cherish to this day. Her family generously shared their country home and included me in many of their family vacations and activities. They also provided abundantly for my family by giving us food and gifts, making clothes, and providing childcare for my siblings and me. They were quiet, wise, yet modest folks who found happiness in service. If there ever was one family I would have turned to in my youth for help, it would have been them, but I couldn't bear the thought of disappointing them. They loved me and had done so much for my family that I felt it would have crushed them to learn of my father's wicked sins. They were too dear for me to taint them with my ugly story.

The Goodmans gave me so much more than a safe home, friendship, and delicious food. Though they were people of few words, their lives preached volumes. They always measured people's worth by the quality of their character rather than the size of their bank account or material wealth. Rather than indulging in material things, they received their joy in giving and doing for others. They knew God long before my father came to minister at their church, for they lived off their land and felt His bounty and goodness for years. Their example of strong commitment to family values, friendships, and their faith gave me a glimpse in my early years of what were the most important things in life. Those attributes grew in my heart and became the guide I would eventually follow throughout my adulthood. Their influence impacted my life in a wonderful way, and through them I had a glimpse at how a partnership in a marriage worked. However, it would be years before I would begin to draw on their example and develop the same strength in our marriage.

From families like the Goodmans, I have learned the importance of creating good memories. They can become the "gifts" that tide people over during difficult times. Gestures of kindness, however simple they may seem, create wonderful memories for others. I look back and recognize how my life was enhanced by selfless acts of special people, particularly the Goodman's, who gave me wonderful memories during my childhood, a most valued gift. Their example has taught me to never waste an opportunity to do a special kindness for a child. It may be their greatest legacy.

Jim and I always wanted a large family, for we both
loved children; however, when we tried to have children,
we found it just didn't happen. During the first year of
marriage, I took birth control pills. The higher dose pills
given back then produced large cysts on both of my
ovaries, and after only eleven months of marriage, I
required major surgery to have them removed. It was a
long procedure. When the doctor finally came out from the
operating room, he told my husband he had had to take out
all of the right ovary and 90% of the left one. The large
cysts were nearly impossible to separate from the ovaries;
consequently, I was left with only 10% of one non-working
ovary. The doctor hoped it would begin to function and
release eggs someday. Brother, so did we! That was a
shocker, but our invincible youth mixed a lot of hope with
that dismal news, and thankfully, within three years, I was
pregnant with our first child.

November 24,1968, our first daughter, Joanna, was
born. She was definitely the most beautiful dark-haired,
olive-skinned baby I had ever seen. (A proud mother
speaking.) What Jim remembers vividly is that she had a
pointed head, and as a first-time father, he was afraid it
might be a permanent deformity. A week later, he was
much relieved when her head took on a normal shape.

As I held our precious child in my arms, I promised
her that I would guard her with my life and never allow a
sinful act to touch her. I spent the next years diligently
living out my promise. One way I thought I was
accomplishing this was to encourage her to be assertive and
independent, because I wanted to make sure she would
never take any form of abuse from anyone. Little did I
realize that she needed very little help in that area, for she
was born with a healthy dose of strong will and learned to
hold her own very early in life. It would have been helpful
to Joanna and all my children if I were stronger-willed

myself and more assertive. But sadly, I wasn't there yet. I was still tied up with my own issues regarding my upbringing. I was programmed not to trust my instincts and to let others control the situation. *Others* often became my children.

Joanna survived six years of her overprotective mother before our second daughter was born. We had been told by doctors that we would probably not have any more children because of my infertility problem, so when our second daughter Elizabeth came along, we were ecstatic. Joanna was delighted to have a sister, even if she was a redhead, and she insisted on sleeping in the same room with Elizabeth and caring for her all she could. Two and a half years later, and *much to our surprise* and the doctors', we were blessed to have a third daughter. In October 1977, our precious Diane was born. Our three daughters completed our family. I have always considered our beautiful daughters three wonderful miracles.

Immediately after the birth of Elizabeth, I developed extremely high blood pressure, which caused my body to go into a series of grand mal seizures. My physician told me the convulsions and high blood pressure were the result of Elizabeth's short labor and delivery time, which was fifteen minutes. From the thrashing of the seizures, I chewed my tongue raw, my arms were black and blue from broken blood vessels, and I had ripped apart the stitches from my episiotomy. I lay unconscious for twelve hours. My doctor feared I might never come out of the coma, and if I did, he thought I might have long-term consequences. It took a while to recover from that ordeal. My problems were compounded by frequent nightmares, migraine headaches, postpartum depression, and kidney problems. I now have only one working kidney.

Because of all these challenges, Jim had more than his share of work. For many years, he would have to come home early to care for either the children or me, and then return later that evening to work in order to make up for the lost time. He had changed careers from teaching to banking in Cadillac, Michigan.

A tender moment I often recall is seeing Jim kneeling by my bedside during one of my terrible migraine headache episodes. They were so bad I didn't think I could live through another one. Jim came into our darkened bedroom and knelt by my side. With his hands folded, he prayed earnestly for my healing. My loving husband caressed my head, kissed me tenderly, and said, "I wish you didn't have these, Pumpkin." I was deeply moved. I knew that my headaches were a concern to him, as well as a burden, for his workload had doubled during those years.

Jim insisted I see a doctor, because the headaches were so severe and frequent. At my appointment, all I could tell the doctor about my excruciating headaches was that they always came on in the middle of the night and lasted 24 to 36 hours. During that time, I would vomit so hard that I would temporarily lose my vision. Even for health reasons, I could not uncover the ugly wound that kept weeping within. Tests were ordered, and they revealed I had an allergy to gluten, an ingredient that is in wheat, rye, oats, and bran. I was sent to see a dietitian and learned to eat gluten-free meals, but the headaches persisted. However, the new diet made them less intense. At least now I had an alibi for the cruel midnight invaders, which allowed me to keep my shameful secret hidden for another fifteen years.

Because of my compromised health, the last two children received less smothering and mothering from me. With the help of my husband, they survived nicely.

Coming to terms with my own dysfunction and learning to operate as a healthy adult was a challenge. This took time and didn't fully happen until our three children were mostly raised, which brought difficulties on the home front. What the children said and wanted quickly triggered the compliance channel in my mind to do as I was told. Consequently, Jim became involved in much of the disciplining at home. I remember him asking me, "Shirl, why are you letting them do that? Remember, you're the adult here, the one in charge." Jim's suggestions not only made me aware of my problem, but also facilitated the needed changes in me. I found myself repeating Jim's words, "Remember I'm the adult here, so I need to take charge and do what is right." New thought patterns and habits take time.

As our three girls reached the same age I was when I was sexually abused, my anger for my father and my mother worsened. I remember thinking, "How could any father ever touch his own flesh and blood in any other way than what is pure?" Our little girls were precious, and I thought, "Wasn't I just as precious?" They were my little angels, and I knew I would protect them any way I could— even with my life. I guarded them carefully when they were around men and taught them to be strong and independent by reinforcing that they did not have to take anything from any man if they did not want to. I wanted them to use their strong voices at home when they were angry so they knew how to scream whenever in trouble. I often reinforced these behaviors to the extreme, especially with my firstborn. I also told them to find a husband just like their dad.

Because of the cool relationship I had with my mother, I did not know how to relate well on an emotional level, with my daughters. I needed help in that area. Little talks or going out for walks or lunch never happened while I grew up, and it took time before I realized their importance and began to incorporate them with my own daughters. Bonding through good times and bad is what glues families, especially mothers to daughters. We relate through talking and sharing, so there need to be lots of opportunities for that. Thank heavens it's never too late to begin developing a loving, authentic relationship with our children. There is no better gift or support team than family members who love you. My daughters are so dear, and I make a conscious effort to be a good mom. Cell phones and email have become wonderful aids. Our children are precious at any age, and they deserve the best we can give them. If you are blessed to have children, I hope you connect with them at a heart-level regularly.

Jim adapted quickly to fatherhood. His love and caring nature for the girls reassured me that I never had to worry about him abusing our girls. Their personal privacy was of utmost importance to him, and respect was his way of life. I smiled as I saw his love in action toward our girls, such a contrast from my father. He also gave me strokes of confidence and praise, and freedom to think for myself. His example of truth, courage, and patience became wonderful patterns to follow.

As I emotionally matured, it added a healthy balance to our marriage. The more I took charge of my emotional health, the more I was able to wisely handle the responsibilities at home. I also feel comfortable in saying that I was given natural mothering traits, for I love my children profoundly. There were many areas in parenting in which I could have done better if I had been healthier, and I have regrets in those areas. My sister Georgia reminded me that all parents have regrets, no matter how they raise their children. My brother-in-law Paul's words, "You did the very best you possible could at the time," also helped to ease my mind. Regrets are something we need to release. Dwelling on them only wastes time and drains our energy.

We are thankful that our daughters are healthy, wonderful young women who love us so much. They each radiate in their own special way in spite of their personal challenges. Yes, our family is not without our share of problems. We are glad they are women of faith, and their kind hearts and positive attitudes make them especially beautiful people. We are so proud of them. It's hard to be humble.

We were given a bonus daughter in 1977 when our foster daughter, Susan, came to live with us at the age of fifteen. Her mother had died suddenly from a heart attack when Susan was twelve. One summer afternoon, her father came to visit us and asked if we wanted another daughter, for he was unable to care for her any longer. We had met Susan in 1968 when we first moved to Mesick. Her family lived right next door to us, making it easy for me to babysit Susan. I cared for her for the next four years. Joanna was only eleven months old at that time, and Susan always considered Joanna to be her little sister. It was an easy decision to add her to our family, and she has been a delightful addition.

An ongoing problem I continued to have was relating in a healthy manner with the opposite sex. For years, I didn't think I had anything worth offering men but my sex appeal. My father's early influence convinced me that a woman's sexuality is all men want or value in a woman, anyway. I struggled with my sexuality and my desire for other men. I didn't understand then how my abuse contributed to my relational problems with men. I was so handicapped in knowing how to relate healthy with other men. I look back now and thank God that nothing ever materialized from that behavior and that I was spared from having extramarital affairs. Sexual promiscuity is a problem that commonly accompanies sexually abused victims, and when that happens, it brings additional heartaches, *especially* if one is married.

It was reassuring when I finally gained a sense of worth and realized that I certainly had much more to offer than my sexuality and began to display it in a healthy manner. I am not a target any longer for anyone looking for a flirtatious friendship; in fact, I become offended if any man makes even the slightest sensual suggestion.

My newfound confidence brought along a companion: assertiveness. This new attitude gave me courage to speak out on many subjects, especially about injustices. When I first found my voice, I was so happy to finally be able to talk about issues that were close to my heart that I would often broadcast wrongs, without even thinking ahead. True, wrongs need to be brought into the light, but not with arrogance. How humbling. I've since learned to hesitate before I speak, and to pick my words carefully. The words we choose determine our effectiveness, and I've found that a few well-chosen words are usually more effective.

Telling my daughters about the incest made them wiser to the world regarding sexual abuse. As difficult as it was to talk about the abuse, it opened the door for further talks on many issues that concerned them. I hope this book does the same for other parents, and encourages them to talk about incest or sexual abuse before it happens to their children.

Giving our children the freedom to talk about sex is a safety net they need to have. In fact, the whole intriguing topic of sex and their sexuality needs to be discussed. Sex and reproduction are very normal and exciting parts of life, and should be viewed and respected with the importance they hold. Likewise, incest and sexual abuse need to be defined for children in a way they will understand, and told that it is wrong. They won't know if we don't tell them.

One woman I worked with said as a young child, she didn't know that incest was bad. She knew she didn't like it, but it was something she had to do. She thought all children had to.

Sexually abused victims unfortunately are dished an ugly, distorted picture of what sexual relations between two people should be. Victims are therefore robbed of the beauty and enjoyment that is meant to accompany sexual intimacy. *Incest steals from children their innocence before they have the opportunity to figure out their sexuality.* Speaking from experience, this unhealthy view of sex is difficult to change. The impressions made upon us in our youth are powerful images that are hard to remove.

Working at the health department provides me with opportunities to remain abreast of many health concerns, especially sexually transmitted diseases. Holly, the nurse practitioner with whom I work, reminded me that eight out of ten sexually active persons carry a sexual transmitted disease (STD), and many of them don't realize it. That terribly high percentage is why she strongly advocates abstinence until marriage, and believes it is the only hope our single people have if they want to stay free from STDs. Too many diseases are epidemic in our society.

I would add another reason for being abstinent until we find that special person to spend the rest of our life with, and that is for our emotional well-being. Sex has a way of bonding us to the partner with whom we are intimate, especially for women. When that relationship breaks, so does our heart—leaving scars. When this pattern is repeated, it becomes hard to bond with anyone, for the scarring of our hearts prohibits further attachments.

At a book signing in a mall recently a man approached me and asked if I addressed the issue of sibling sexual abuse in my book. His older brother had sexually abused him for many years while growing up. He felt he had to comply with his brother's wishes or face physical and emotional abuse by him. To this day, he grieves over the sexual acts his brother coerced him into doing and often suffers from mental flash backs. Because of their sorted secret past, he and his brother are estranged. His heart aches to hear his brother say, "I'm sorry, I shouldn't have made you do the things I did". He yearns for restitution in their relationship. He wants to love his brother.

This same story repeats itself all too frequently among siblings, cousins, step siblings, and etc, and because it does, it leaves deep wounds and broken relationships that need to be healed.

Admitting our wrongs and asking for forgiveness are marvelous healing balms that need to be used liberally whenever we screw up. This is especially true when sexual abuse occurs. What the (now adult) child abuser needs to understand is; the sexual involvement he or she created often causes further serious problems that need to be worked out.

Talking about the past will be helpful and healing for both involved, for the truth will set them both free. The sibling or relation who initiated the abuse needs to be the first to say, "I'm sorry. What I did was wrong." If that doesn't happen, it is appropriate for the adult victim to confront the abuser in a safe environment, and discuss the issue. However, this rarely takes place because pride and shame get stuck in the way, and that is very unfortunate.

Whenever I have been told a discussion like this has taken place, the relations between the two have improved greatly. Owning up to our mistakes-*even those we didn't realize were wrong at the time,* is a mark of maturity and wisdom, and greatly helps the one we have injured.

I need to emphasize again the importance of educating our children about sex. They need to know what appropriate and inappropriate sexual behavior is early in life. We need to remind them again as they grow older. Talking about it once won't do it. When we talk about abuse and other sensitive topics with our children, they will feel comfortable coming to us if they occur. And when they do, we should embrace our children and love them unconditionally and not place shame on them.

This is the time to praise them for talking about what has happened. As they see how we handle the situations, they will learn how to confront and resolve difficult issues. They will watch us make that phone call, or set up a meeting. They need to see us protect and rescue them. They are children and are not yet skilled at knowing how to handle difficult issues-especially sexual abuse.

If your child is the one who caused the pain you need to address the wrong with them, and make him or her take responsibility for what they have done. They need to be educated about sexual abuse and told how wrong it is. They also need to apologize to the one they offended. The child needs to know you disliked their hurtful behavior, not them. Once the child has owned up and made amends, you need to remind them how much you love him or her, and that their redeeming actions have given you reason to be very proud of them.

Sexual abuse among children can have devastating affects, yet, healing is also obtainable for them. Addressing difficult issues can be hard to do, because of our examples; I know it was for me. We need to be strong and confront evil, *especially* when it is done to our children. Our children are precious gifts and their care and health is our responsibility.

Being sexually abused is one thing, but when sexual abuse touches your child, it brings a whole new bushel of heartache. Unfortunately, our youngest was a victim of sexual abuse, and she has given me permission to tell the following story.

During the summer months of her college years, Diane was employed at a restaurant as a waitress and a hostess. One evening, while being the friendly hostess, she offered to help a partially blind 70-year-old man find his way to the door after his dinner. The old man purposely grabbed and groped her. She repeatedly yelled at him to stop, but he refused. Finally, she freed herself by pushing him away, nearly throwing him on the floor. She ran away from the scene and into the kitchen of the restaurant, completely humiliated. She rushed home to tell us about her horrible ordeal. You can imagine how angry we were at the man. Courageously, she took him to court and testified how he publicly and physically attacked her. Through investigating, we were told he had raped other girls. That bit of information only fueled her desire to stop him from continuing his perverted behavior. The old geezer has died now, but before he did, he learned that your sins do find you out, and you can't always get away with taking advantage of women, even if you are financially well off and influential. He died a shamed man. I was proud of Diane for not letting him get away with his behavior. Testifying in court wasn't easy, and there were tears, but she persevered. Every woman who has gone through similar situations salutes you, Diane. I only wish I had been as strong and brave at her age. Diane gave up working as a hostess and waitress. She became a lifeguard, and she now has her Master's in family counseling.

ABOVE: Shirley's Miracle Daughters.

BELOW: Three daughters and foster daughter.

Shirley and daughters, in birth order, with foster daughter.

"My Vow"

♥

Look down upon my chest
And gaze into this tiny angel face.
A piece of Heaven has come down
To bless our humble earthly place.
In the womb of this mortal maid
God formed a child of beauty and grace.

I vow to never ever allow
A sinful act to touch her brow
Or lie beside and crush her flesh,
Not this Child that heaven sent.
Though only with me for a little while,
With my life I'll guard my precious child.

SJP

14

Healing from the inside requires learning to forgive oneself.

Cheryl, an acquaintance of mine, told me she had been carrying guilt because, during her sexual abuse, she began to experience sexual pleasure. She struggled with a terrible inner conflict of hating him, but also enjoying the physical experience. I explained to her that sexual abuse can be and often is pleasurable for the victim. Many sex offenders want their victim to enjoy sex so the molestation can continue without a struggle. Our bodies are made to respond to sexual stimulation, and as I told her, there is no need for guilt. Sexual pleasure is a natural human response given to us.

I remember my father telling me, "Just enjoy it." He would take extra time trying to get me to respond to his unwanted touch. He said that he wanted to teach me to have an orgasm, a word I didn't even comprehend at the time. This is when I used a diversion so I would purposefully not respond to him. I would chant cheers, louder and louder, in my thoughts. At least I could refuse to cooperate in that matter. Besides, I couldn't get past the disgusting acts, and the fact that it was my father doing them to me. However, I can understand the complexity of Cheryl's issue.

Many victims have told me they learned to enjoy sex very young from their abuser, which unfortunately led them down a long dark road of being promiscuous.

We have to remember that we were victimized and made to do things that we would never do under our own power. I advised her to give herself time and to release her guilt, and to get into counseling. It may take her a longer time to recover. I also urged her to give this situation up to God and tell Him how badly she felt, and to forgive herself and to let it go. God helps us to make peace with ourselves.

I love the verses in which Jesus said, "Come to me, all you who are weary and burdened, and I will give you rest. Take my yoke upon you and learn from me, for I am gentle and humble in heart and you will find rest for your souls. For my yoke is easy and my burden is light" (Matthew 11: 28-30). These verses say we can always come to the Lord and give Him our every concern, our worries, our filth and pain, because *God loves us* and wants to carry our burdens for us. God wants to be our Father in every good sense of the word.

The loving, *Good Father* concept was something I needed to cultivate until I was convinced of its truth. I had to read up and meditate upon that thought until it finally sunk in. Because of my earthly father's behavior, it took time to understand the depth of my Heavenly Father's love for me.

In my continuing search to find ways to get over my sexual abuse, I heard an interesting sermon. A minister read a verse in the Bible that said I should start praying for my abuser. Well, I knew my father needed help, but at that time, I was secretly hoping bad things would happen to him to make up for all he did to me. Now I was to pray for

God's blessing on him. "Pray for those who persecute you" (Matthew 5:44).

I reluctantly took that idea to heart. I did it because I was willing to do anything that would help me put my ugly past behind me. I came to the conclusion that we all need to pray for those who hurt us for if they feel blessed and loved, their attitude and actions can't help but improve.

I found in the process of praying for my abuser that my heart began to change as well. It softened and allowed me to be open for more ideas and changes, all which helped me to overcome my hatred and shamefulness. Although I was reluctant to pray, I found prayer changes things. It changed my heart. You can't hate someone you pray for for long.

I can honestly say that my hate for my father has been dissolved, and the shame from the incest is completely gone. I have shared with you the depth of my hate and shame, so you can understand when I tell you what a gift it is to have those burdens removed. Because I am so free, I find it easy to share my story with others.

One person said to me, "In your autobiography, your life will be in print. Are you sure you want this known about you?" My answer to her was, "Why not? The embarrassment and shame lays with my father, not me."

What happened to me in my youth has no bearing on my worth. I am so convinced of that that I gladly tell my story to anyone. I am free from what my father did to me, and from any guilt that was associated with it. Whenever I revisit my past, I realize that incest was a very unfortunate part of it. However, today is the present, the most important time in my life, and I refuse to let the ghosts of my past destroy any part of it.

Even if your abuser has died, it is still important to free yourself from the negative effects they have upon you. Hate for another individual, whether alive or dead, is never part of a healthy mind. Saying the words, "I am letting this go," is a giant step in the recovery process, even if the abuser has died. Freedom over hate is always a wise choice.

My friend Rachel asked me to remind her what the benefits were to forgiving When we choose to forgive we place our problems in higher hands and let God take care of the problem. We park our problems forever with God so bitterness won't poison us.

When I was plagued with memories of my abuse, I would remind myself to let it go, forgive and go on. This had to become a habit. When your pain and shame lessen, it becomes easier to accept the concept of forgiveness. Some preach you have to forgive while you are still in horrible emotional pain and you can't imagine the idea. When we allow others to love us and minister to us, our pain goes and then we become more open to the idea of forgiveness. When you can forgive your abusers and yourself you have jumped a huge hurtle on your healing journey. It is usually our stubbornness that prohibits our healing.

When I *let it go*, I refuse to allow myself to dwell on the person who caused the problem. This allows me *not* to be controlled by that person. Some situations are so painful that the only way I can do this is to place my problems in "higher hands". I park my problem in God's hands so bitterness won't poison me. When I was plagued with memories of my abuse, I would often tell myself to *let it go*. I would mentally lift them up and give them to God. Then I would go busy myself with an activity such as making music. That allowed me to move past the difficult moment and get on with my life rather than to dwell in my misery.

Forgiveness finally came when I was able to put my situation in its *final resting place*. This took considerable time. Forgiving my father and mother was a process that began by me telling my story and allowing others to shine light on the truth about my story. That allowed my spirit the freedom to pursue that journey. On my healing journey I needed a lot of questions answered, and I needed to figure out what forgiving meant. Once that happened, and with *God's help*, forgiveness began to take place.

When my father repented and asked me to forgive him. I told him, "I forgive you." After that time, I noticed that the ugly memories began to fade away permanently.

I am one of the fortunate victims who had everything finally came into play concerning my abuse. My father confessed to his sins, and then repented and asked me to forgive him. I was able to forgive him and experience healing from the rippling affect from my abuse. I realize I have had it easy compared to many victims who never hear their abuser confess to their crimes or hear "I'm sorry. Please forgive me." To you dear ones, I believe there is a special blessing waiting from God if you pursue truth and healing. God will fill your yearning heart with affirmation and peace. And I believe we sojourners have an important role in assisting God in doing that.

15

Let your standards leave you standing tall.

It would be a mistake for me to tell only about the dark side of my father Martin Lillie, because I believe that no one is completely bad, and that certainly includes him. For a long time, it was hard for me to see him in any kind of positive light because of our sordid history. My father considered himself a child of God, yet he called his sins demons. Just before I made the move to leave home, I think my father was beginning to feel some remorse for his perverted actions. I remember him coming into my bedroom one morning after a late night episode and telling me that he felt badly, but couldn't stop the sexual abuse. He told me he thought he had a demon inside him. After his remarks, I offered to pray with him to cast the demon out. I had heard of missionaries doing that sort of thing before, and I was willing to give it a try. He scoffed at the idea and left my room.

While he was abusing me, I begged him many times to get help. He despised my gestures and became more aggressive than normal. My father was truly in a pitiful state, for how much power or enjoyment could be derived from abusing your own helpless daughter?

I firmly believe that he refused to work on his problems because of his inability to trust people, a product of his abusive past, and because he did not want to give up the things that made him feel better. He needed that feeling of power and pleasure to compensate for his weakness and pain. I also believe he did it just because he could. I heard President Clinton state about his affair with Monica Lewinsky, that one reason he did it was because he could. I believe it was the same with my father.

I often thought it would have been easier to forgive my father if he was an alcoholic, or a drug addict, for then I would have had something to blame his actions on. But he wasn't. He was sober when he abused me. The only excuse I could come up with for my father was that he had a sick mind. That conclusion wasn't very pretty, but it was reality.

In spite of his shortcomings, my father had redeeming qualities. He was a man of vision with a creative edge, and he accomplished a great deal of good for many troubled youth across America. After he resigned from being the pastor at the Plainwell church, he devoted his time to creating faith-based ministries to help direct misguided youth and their families. He had a special place in his heart for troubled teens especially, because he himself had been one. He developed a Christian boarding school in Grand Rapids, Michigan (the organization is no longer there), and later one in Indiana. Many good things came out of his efforts; many lives were redirected, and many families helped. He, with the help of many supporters, has left a legacy of hope for teens that flourishes today. He also organized a Christian survival camp in Canada and a co-ed Christian boarding school in the West Indies. He had an eye for design and created the plans and the buildings for the campuses. I'm sure he would say, in spite of his shortcomings, some good came out of his life. I would add that *a lot* of good came out of his life.

I feel my mother failed my father in some respects, as she did me. She needed to be his helpmate rather than tolerate or cover up his wrongdoings. It was her right and responsibility to have a voice in such matters. She should have insisted he receive help. Instead she became an enabler for him. I am aware that my father contributed to her weakness, for his brainwashing had a big effect on her, as it did me. Yet, she was an adult and could have made better choices, which would have helped us all.

There are many reasons why we tolerate hurtful behaviors from others, but I believe the God in my Bible never asks us to tolerate abuse in a marriage relationship or elsewhere. If we are caught in a relationship where there is sexual, physical, emotional or spiritual abuse we need to flee from that relationship. God did not create us to be doormats. God deplores all acts of sin and violence, and reinforces our great worth to Him. We are dearly loved children, and God instructs us to love each other, and to treat others with love. God has invested a tremendous amount in us and desires the best life possible for us—the *abundant life.*

My father's story, though uncomfortable to hear, is one from which we can all learn. King David, in the Bible, after committing adultery and then orchestrating a murder, was in agony. The consequences of his sins were unbearable. His most intense pain was from being separated from his God, who was his source of strength, wisdom, and comfort throughout his lifetime. That is why he instructed his children, "Learn from me!" He did not want them to repeat his mistakes and wanted to spare them the agony he experienced. Although my father's sins were of a different nature, I think he would say the same: "Learn from me and don't repeat my mistakes." He often said,

"Regrets are hard to live with. I know because my life has been full of them."

No sin is worth the consequences or the pain it brings. David begged God to forgive him and to take away his anguish. My father also repented and asked for forgiveness, and God's generous mercy covered them both, just as it does each one of us when we come to Him. Mercy is a beautiful example of God's love for us.

As I re-examined my father's life from the perspective of an unwanted, unloved child, to the idea of a man who spent years building refuges for troubled teenagers, I can't but help admire his efforts. With the terrible heartaches he experienced as a child, it is not surprising all the pain he caused others. A loner, he wandered through life, often far from God's ways. I've concluded that for the most part, he could do no better, for he was missing an important link to having a healthy, psychological mind, and that was the unconditional love of parents. He was missing a critical element that every human being needs to thrive, that of *love*. Also, the unfortunate conservative religious teachings of how a wife should relate to her husband prohibited my mother from being the helpmate my father desperately needed.

I can relate somewhat to my father's heartache because of the pain I endured. However, my outcome was much different, because, though I didn't have the love and support I needed from my parents, I was fortunate to have the unconditional love and support of a husband and children, along with friends, and later my siblings. I had a whole support system that loved me (and I loved them as well), which helped me to stay on course.

My father needed forgiveness, but he also needed love. He needed it badly years ago. An important reminder in all of this is how crucial love is to our emotional growth and self-image, especially the love of our caregivers.

During the 1990's, I worked with young mothers and reminded them that more important than the formula they fed their infants, was the holding and love they imparted to them. We encouraged breastfeeding not only for the nutritional benefits, but also for the bond that it creates between mom and baby. Love is essential for our existence.

My father's time for being loved has passed; however, I hope his tragic story will remind us of how very important it is to truly love our children. If we can't love them, allow someone else who can. *Children deserve all the love they can get.*

I believe with all my heart, that under different circumstances my father never would have abused me. If he had been loved and nurtured properly, the incest would never have happened, for there would have been no need for him to commit such sins.

There are times I fantasize about the father he should have been. I visualize him enjoying his children and grandchildren, genuinely interested in each one. I can envision him standing proud at graduations and beaming at weddings. That's the father I could have had if things had been different for him, and at the end of his life, that's the father I like to believe he was starting to become.

The last time I saw my father alive, I witnessed a genuine humility. His eyes and face were filled with remorse. He told me he was proud of his children, and that he did love us. With tears in his eyes, he admitted to me that he was a horrible father and asked me once again to forgive him. He said that all his kids deserved a better father than he was. I know that even though he asked for God's mercy, his last days were not easy. But now, at last, he's experiencing the unconditional love of a Heavenly Father, love he needed so long ago.

It was a tragedy that my father did not seek counseling much earlier. He often counseled others and knew of its importance. Maybe shame was the reason for him, as it was for me. If he had received counseling, who knows what even greater things he might have accomplished?   He had such potential.   Loving surroundings and wise therapy would have helped to alleviate his pain, which would have ended his need to abuse others emotionally, physically, or sexually. As I said earlier, sharing one's deep hurts is so important. My father needed to find someone to talk to long ago. How I wish he had, for both our sakes.

16

No matter what you're told, you are not wrecked for life... only painfully wiser than most

The more I talk with others about incest, the more I realize just how prevalent this crime is. I have heard speakers quote statistics saying that one in six females and one in four males become victims of sexual abuse before the age of eighteen. I maintain that the numbers are much higher. Sexual abuse is a *huge* problem in our society, and what makes incest especially nauseating is that the predators are family members—those who are supposed to love you. I've heard so many sad stories from victims about how a brother, an uncle, a father, a grandparent, a step relative, or even a godparent had sexually abused them.

Sexual abuse and the shame that accompanies it can destroy one's self-worth and quality of life, and leave wounds that fester for a lifetime. That is why I am convinced that promiscuity, alcoholism, drug addictions, and other abusive behaviors are so high. We victims will use any means available to numb our pain, or allow us to escape from our horrible memories.

The only reason I hesitate in telling my story is because my perpetrator was a minister. By exposing his sins, it opens up the Christian faith to more ridicule, and that is unfortunate. It seems the Christian faith already gets more than its share of negative press. However, if we are ignorant to the hypocrisy in religion, and ignore or protect those who abuse their religious privileges, our faith institutions will keep losing ground.

The truth is, sexual sins happen everywhere, even within the church, and that does not make it any more tolerable. In fact, the church is the first place it needs to be eradicated. I can't imagine anything that would anger God more than committing sexual sins against His children under the cross that bears His name. Yet, sadly, we continue to hear reports that sexual sins persist behind the doors of those who are labeled "men of God" or "leaders of our faith".

Another tragedy is that, because sexual abuse has become such a common occurrence in our society, it rarely shocks us anymore. Our children are more vulnerable today than ever, and I believe our changing family dynamics, declining moral values, easy access to pornographic material, and the lack of connection and supervision by those who are children's primary caretakers all add to this serious problem.

While working in a women's health clinic, I met a lovely seventeen-year-old girl named Tonya who had been a victim of incest. She was originally from Mexico, but an American family adopted her at birth. Her adoptive parents divorced when she was ten years old. A few years later, her mother remarried. Shortly afterwards, her stepfather began to sexually abuse her. By the time I met her, she had not seen her mother for three years. Her mother was still angry with her for squealing on her stepfather and for having him put in jail. Tonya was living with relatives, because her mother would have nothing to do with her. Her stepfather received only eighteen months in prison for his offense. I held her arm tenderly that day as I took her blood pressure. Oh, how I wanted to hug her and take her home. In her weary dark eyes, I could sense the pain and confusion that poor child was experiencing, and my heart ached for her. I can only imagine the hurt and heavy burden she continues to bear.

Doesn't it make you wonder who has any sense or values nowadays? Have we become a society so lacking in morals that we don't even protect our young any more? *Tonya's story is not an isolated case.* Unfortunately, similar stories happen all too frequently. I have heard many alarming stories of how mothers ignore situations, and that angers me. It makes me wonder how many of them have been likewise sexually abused. Being aware of Tonya's story and realizing the commonness of sexual abuse helps one to understand why children endure such pain and keep the terrible secrets to themselves. They face the ultimate risk of losing both parents, so they keep silent and endure the pain. This should never happen.

I came across an interesting scenario regarding a twelve -year-old daughter who was a victim of incest. Her father would reward her with gifts for allowing him to abuse her. He would often take her shopping after he sexually abused her and let her buy whatever she wanted. She obliged her father easily, for it became a good tradeoff. When her mother learned of the sexual abuse, she was furious and put a stop to it; however, the daughter got angry with her mother, for she loved all the "perks" she was receiving. How interesting!

We need to do all we can to educate and protect our children. Their lives and future happiness depend on *us*.

I have told you that I have no more bitterness or pain from my incest experience, and that is true. Yet, when I see others who are struggling with similar issues, I can look back and remember a time when I was in their shoes and deeply empathize with them. I can relate to the agony they are going through, and I wish I could help them even more.

For eight years, I worked as a certified vision technician for the heath department and screened students for vision impairments within the school systems. This included all ninth grade students. I remember a particularly troubling day in the fall of 1998. While setting up my equipment, I couldn't help but notice what was transpiring in the principal's office just across the hall from me. His door was open far enough for me to see a tall, lean ninth grade girl sitting in front of him. Her long brown hair was pulled back in a ponytail that dangled down her thin back. Her shoulders and head were slumped downward as she stared at the carpeted floor. I could hear that she was receiving a scolding from the principal for being tardy, and I assessed that this had been a frequent occurrence. She sat mute and motionless as she accepted her verbal punishment. I couldn't help but wonder about the reason she was so often tardy.

I felt a connection with her as my mind flashed back to a time when I, too, was in her situation. The nights were short during those years I was sexually abused, and I was often tardy, for I could hardly get myself out of bed on those mornings. I also sat mute many times in front of my principal, not daring to tell why this continued to happen.

Repeated tardiness is not something teenagers enjoy, for it is very embarrassing. Rather, it could be a symptom of an underlying problem that is out of their control. Being intuitive is an important skill that educators and administrators need to possess. Finding the source of the problem is the key to finding the cure, a common yet true statement.

This is just one example of how our societies, even our school systems, are naively unaware of the prevalence of sexual abuse or the consequences it brings. We wonder why depression, sexual and drug addictions, and suicides continue to escalate. The results of sexual abuse are life altering and can be devastating. As you read the following list of consequences from sexual abuse, I think you will agree with me that we need to do something to stop this epidemic from destroying our children. This list was compiled after talking with many victims, and includes the following outcomes:

- A distorted value system of what is right and wrong.
- Vulnerability in relationships.
- Inability to relate to men/women in a healthy manner.
- Accelerated unhealthy sexual behaviors.
- Stunted emotional growth.
- Low self-esteem.
- Isolation, forced into solitude, loneliness.
- Sexual dysfunction, sexual obsession.
- Patterns of telling lies.
- Dependence on the abuser.
- Exposure to sexually transmitted diseases, pregnancy, and urinary tract infections.
- Anxiety and fatigue.
- Food related illnesses (i.e., anorexia, bulimia).
- Drug and alcohol addictions.
- Poor attendance, tardiness, and low performance in school and work.
- Depression, headaches, feeling cold and numb.
- Sleep deprivation and/or nightmares.
- Self torture—physical abuse and suicidal traits.

The list is sobering. I can testify, as a victim, to its validity, for I experienced many of these effects myself and know how difficult it is to overcome the serious consequences that can follow sexual abuse. One particular young gal used *cutting* as a means of relieving her emotional pain. She would take razor blades and make slits across her inner arm. When I asked her how it helped, her response was, "Watching the blood flow out from my body somehow takes my pain away."

With problems such as the ones listed, it is no wonder victims of incest and sexual abuse struggle to find meaning in life. It is important that we find ways to expose those who are committing sexual abuse and stop this terrible sin against all humankind. I hope that by speaking out against incest, and by making the public aware of its serious consequences, I will help to accomplish this goal.

Shirley Erena Murray's moving lyrics to the song "God Weeps" describes well the deep compassion and concern God has towards his children who are abused.

God weeps at love withheld, strength misused,
  at children's innocence abused.
God bleeds at anger's fist, trust betrayed, for women (and children), battered and afraid.
God waits for stones to melt, peace to seed,
  for hearts to hold each other's needs.

Elaine is a girl I met at a church where I was invited to speak and play my music. She was relating her sexual abuse story to me when she commented that she was having a terrible time ridding herself of the filth she felt. She said that she could never get clean enough to rid herself of that awful dirty feeling. That is a problem victims have, and one I too, had to work through. Incest is a dark degrading act, and all the soap in the world can't clean the black scars it leaves. The phenomenon of sexual abuse is the victim somehow caries the shame and filth that belongs to the abuser. We need to let that shame go and realize we were a victim, and none of the abuse was our fault. Children don't want sex, only love, and they are incapable of stopping abuse.

We can never turn back the clock. I can never change what happened to me, but I did find a scrub that removes the black scum so I could feel clean again. Once I started talking about the incest, allowed others to love and help me, and made the effort to forgive my father, time worked its miracle.

There were times when I found myself thinking, "But if I only would have done this, maybe..." No, I've learned those are wasted thoughts.

As I began to believe that I am a person of worth, and loved by family, friends, and God regardless of my past, I didn't feel dirty anymore.

Another biggie that helped me clean up was going to God and confessing my sins. I had my share outside of the abuse. I had to confess and also ask others I had offended to forgive me. Coming cleaned helped me feel clean. Confession is good for the soul. Truth took awhile to sink in, however, I finally realized I had nothing to feel dirty about; after all I was coerced and forced into participating. I was a child and responded like a child. I didn't have the wisdom or strength at that time to have done any differently. I have learned that I am loved and valued for who I am, and what my father did to me does not detract from my worth one bit.

Years ago, I was given a little book entitled *As A Man Thinketh* by James Allen. In it, he reminds us that circumstances do not make the person. However, circumstances can greatly influence us to become someone different than we first planned. How we see ourselves, what we think of ourselves, affects our image and our outlook. We do become what we think we are. If we think we are dirty or worthless, we will most likely act out that attitude and do things that reflect our feelings, even if it is to our detriment. Those destructive behaviors can end up hurting not only our lives, but also the lives of others.

It's important to rid ourselves of the filth and negative thoughts that accompany sexual abuse. Negative words are poison to our spirit and can destroy any hope of happiness. We need to start seeing ourselves in the light in which God does. In God's eyes, we are loveable and worthy of every dream. God's love is most often reflected through the good people he puts in our lives, and we must trust them and lean on their wisdom. We need to absorb all the love they offer, and allow them to instruct us. When we feel loved, our crust of low self-esteem begins to crumble away, which allows us to start loving ourselves. A healthy and beautiful spirit evolves as we learn to accept and love ourselves—which in turn, allows us to love others.

As my self-worth improved, I started taking better care of myself. I started looking people in the eye. I also began to walk with an air of confidence. The smile on my face became genuine, and the more I smiled, I began to notice the world smiled back.

There is hope for everyone, for the shame and low self-esteem that accompany sexual abuse can be eliminated. *We should never think of ourselves as damaged goods or wasted, for that is simply never the case.*

17

Life can be a picnic if you remember to bring the dessert.

While in nursing school some thirty years ago, I was taught that pain is a good thing. It is a symptom, an indicator that something in our body is amiss. Physical pain is a wake-up call telling us to attend to a particular problem within our body so we can experience optimum health. If we avoid seeking professional help, we can often diagnose our problem wrongly. Some of us put a bandage over a sore that needs serious consideration, or we hope our ailments will just go away in time.

I've learned that emotional pain is a condition that needs attention just as our physical pain does. Emotional pain can also magnify our physical illnesses. In fact, it is often the source of our physical ailments. That was something I was naively unaware of, or didn't want to believe was true about myself. I had to learn that lesson the hard way after experiencing years of compromised health, as did Jessie, an acquaintance of mine.

Jessie had a painful, burning ache in the pit of her stomach. She suffered silently for a long time, thinking it would some day get better and eventually go away. One day, the pain got so bad she couldn't stand it another moment, and she ended up in the emergency room. By this time, her condition had significantly worsened, and she ended up needing surgery. She recovered after a period of time, but discovered that she soon had another ailment. This cycle seem to repeat itself until her doctor recommended she see a psychologist. During the course of their visits, she was able to disclose a serious issue that had been troubling her for years. As time passed, she found ways to resolve her personal issue, and miraculously, her health seemed to improve. Today, she tells me that she's never felt better in her life.

Jessie's injury is typical of those of us who have deep wounds of the heart. We suffer silently, hoping that the pain will eventually go away by itself and that we'll get better. But the unattended wounds don't go away. They only worsen and cause our bodies to shut down emotionally and physically. It is equally important for us to have surgery of the heart to remove the ugly secrets, the lies, bitterness, and the self-condemnation as it is to tend to our physical ailments. Our recovery can take a while, but the results can also be miraculous.

I can't stress enough the importance of opening up and telling our bitter experience to another. The boomerang effect of ill health from our emotional pain will continue until we recognize what is happening and address the root cause.

Many victims are unable or unwilling to admit to their sexual abuse, or fail to recognize how it has hindered them. To those of you, I say: you are only fooling yourselves, for you cannot keep a flaming dragon hidden forever. Somehow, and at some time, the effects manifest themselves, and they don't go away with age. In fact, they only intensify as we get older. That was true for me, and I also witnessed it while working with the elderly.

During the years I was a home health nurse, I enjoyed listening to my patients while they shared the experiences of their lives. I gathered some valuable information about them as they talked. As I listened, I could soon identify the ones who had some deep-seated, unresolved emotional pain in their lives. The tone of voice and their words and actions told me more than they probably wanted me to know.

One eighty-year-old patient of mine named Helen showed all the symptoms of having been sexually abused. She was anxious, suspicious, and negative about everyone and everything. She did not even trust her children, who loved her. She also had serious phobias. On one occasion, she told me that while her mother worked, she was sent to babysitters. She went on to say, "You should never send your children to babysitters, because you never know what can happen to them, especially if there are men living at the home." She quickly buttoned up and looked out the window. Her words and body language told me she had probably been sexually abused while at the babysitters a long time ago. Seventy-plus years later, Helen was still feeling the pain and suffering from its consequences.

Sexual abuse is horrible and the consequences from it are horrible as well. It needs to be recognized that way.

Helen's generation was raised in the era when life was more difficult. They were taught that when you experienced hardships, you should grin and bear them. Difficulties were just part of life. Those who yearned for sympathy were often seen as being weak, and you certainly would never mention the word *sex* to anyone. Family therapists did not exist in their day, and, because of their phobias, some patients wouldn't accept or trust therapists even today. It is easy to understand how those abused individuals can become hard and bitter, and there seem to be a lot of them around. My heart goes out to that generation. They need to be reached, heard, educated, and embraced.

The saying " Life isn't over till it's over" is certainly true for our older generation as well. The potential for a better life is there for them as well, if they would only take that journey and grab on to the assistance available.

There is another story that I would like to share with you. I met an eccentric, large woman named Dotty through work. She was in her early seventies and did not hesitate to talk about her sexual abuse to anyone. She said that it didn't negatively affect her at all. In fact, it aggravates her when others get hung up on their sexual abuse experience. Her advice to them is that you just need to put it out of your head and get on with your life. Dotty has had three husbands and is a perfectionist. She's self-centered and avoids emotional attachments. She is also suspicious of every man she sees but, *no*, there isn't anything wrong with her, according to her own opinion of herself.

Maybe you also think you have escaped the negative effects of the sexual abuse in your past. Here is a simple list of questions that I have accumulated after talking with many victims. It may help to evaluate how well you are really doing:

- Are there times in your past that you just can't remember or choose to avoid because they are too painful?
- Do you find yourself vulnerable and unable to set boundaries for yourself?
- Do you resist relationships that require commitment, intimacy, and trust?
- Do you have sleeping or eating disorders, or other ailments that just don't go away?
- Do you have low self-esteem and find it difficult to make decisions?

- Do you have compulsive behaviors that are unhealthy?
- Do you have nightmares or hear voices?
- Do you stay away from people and activities because of the fear of what might happen?
- Do you feel the worst is always going to happen?
- Do you find you have tendencies to be promiscuous, or are you sexually driven?
- Are you unhappy and don't like yourself?
- Do you have trust issues?
- Are you often depressed and feel you have little reason to live, or wish you would die?

If you answer yes to any of these questions, you need to re-evaluate yourself and talk to a friend *and a professional.* Your problems could very well stem from the sexual abuse in your past. I urge you to seek help. Look in the phone book and call any counseling center, hotline, church, or synagogue. They can refer you to a reputable counselor.

We are never too young or too old to start talking about what is hurting us.

I have heard it said so many times: "Life is too short to let things bother you." Well, my response to that is, "Life is too long for us to carry around all the heavy burdens from our past." The sooner we face our pain, the happier our lives will become.

If you've been a victim of sexual abuse, remember you are never alone. God is always there for you. He will certainly shine a light on your path so you can find a way out of your misery. Persist. You will experience relief. And believe me, the final outcome is worth your effort. In Deuteronomy 33:8 in the Holy Bible, I read, *"The Lord is the one who goes before you. He will be with you. He will not leave you. Do not fear or be dismayed."*

There will be a day of reckoning. God is the one who said, "Vengeance is mine." I find great comfort knowing God is just, and will judge appropriately those who have done wrong.

We have to expose the evil that was done to us in order for us to experience true freedom from it, and also to eliminate that behavior from happening to others.

Katie, an acquaintance of mine, was ready to leave her husband because he failed to help her with her sexual abuse issues. She told me he was just adding to her frustrations by being non-sympathetic and evasive. She needed more compassion from him and wanted him just to listen to her heartache.

Incest is a terribly sensitive and distasteful subject, even for men. It is even more sensitive when the abuse happens to their wives. I told Katie that her husband was probably going through more than she realized and didn't know how to handle it. He may also have been avoiding the topic further because her pain brings him more pain as well. Also, he possibly could have been sexually abused and can't go anywhere near the topic.

It is true our spouses will never know how much we are affected by the abuse, or how much it has interrupted our marriage, unless they hear us out. I encourage every spouse of a victim to be actively supportive as the victims get through this time of crisis. The subject of incest is very distasteful, yet victims need a support team, and we are supposed to be there for each other as mates. Remember the "In sickness or health" part of our vows? The emotional health of an abused spouse affects the quality of life for their mate, as well as the whole family, so it is imperative that husbands, or wives, take an active, supportive role towards helping them to recover.

There are professionals who specialize in areas that can help you both. Go to counseling with your spouse.

Learn and read together. It's not only important, but both of you will reap the benefits. You will experience a marriage that is better than you ever thought possible, including your sex life. Many rewards are waiting at the end for you. Jim's role was critical in my recovery. His daily affirmation of my innocence and self-worth was monumental. I like to say, he loved me well. Jim's love brought me back to health.

Clark Barshinger and Lajan LaRowe have authored a helpful book to assist spouses on this matter called *Haunted Marriage*. Every husband (or wife) whose spouse has been sexually abused could benefit from this book. The information shared could not only save your marriage, but also take your relationship to heights you never knew existed.

My social worker/counselor brother David reminded me that all husbands aren't perfect. In fact, he said none of us are. His concern is that when others read about Jim, they might feel a bit inadequate in handling issues like incest. He believes that most men don't have the patience or skills to handle such sensitive issues by themselves, and they need to be encouraged to seek professional help. I echo his claim. Professional counseling is important. Counselors have skills and insight that help us get to the core of our problems, which can hasten our recovery time.

I told my husband that he should be the one writing this book, because he has an enormous amount of insight to share with others, particularly with men. But realistically, I don't think that's going to happen, at least not for a while. Jim's gentle spirit is more at home wandering through rolling hills of golden Aspens, or playing cards with family and friends, than at a computer writing a book. However, he takes a big supportive role in helping me, and that means so very much.

One friend said she felt a bit envious as she read about all the support I received from my husband. She asked whether Jim had a brother and, if not, could she clone him for herself? That was a touching tribute to my husband, one that I shared with him. Jim does not want to be portrayed as a saint. He is human and he realizes he has faults. But I can tell you that after being married to him for over 40 years they are very few.

I love movies and books that have a happy ending. They are not only entertaining, but also add an essence of hope to our own life situations. If you leave with anything after reading this book, I trust it has given you hope for your future regardless of your circumstance. As a survivor of sexual abuse, I can tell you that if you persevere, better days are waiting ahead for you.

My friend Kay told me, "Shirley, you are more than a survivor. You prevailed!" I believe the same positive outcome can happen to nearly everyone. It is a matter of recognizing the seriousness of our problem and then being willing to do the necessary steps to remedy our misfortunes. *Life can be sweet!*

"The Dance of Freedom"

From the "taste of freedom" this dance came
Now my liberated heart will never tame
A soul enslaved is forever set free
Life has birthed anew in me.

When freedom chanted at my door
I went with haste, my spirit soared.
Now exalted I'm back again
To help another experience the same.

Oh, come and dance away with me
And let your shame and pain go free
For freedom is life but you'll never know
Lest your fears you release
Come, let's go!

18

I'm moving on. I've cut the cord and left my baggage behind.

There is a story about an old woman who walked every day to the park. She would sit on the same park bench and mutter the same thing each day: "I wish the sun would come out and push these dark clouds away."

A stranger passing by heard the old women's comment and said, "Madam, it's a beautiful sunny day. Take your umbrella down and that dark cloud will go away."

The old lady looked up at the stranger with amazement and replied, "Really? It is a beautiful day?"

The stranger nodded her head and replied, " Yes."

The old lady reached up and struggled to take her umbrella down, but it wouldn't come. It had been up so long that the umbrella had rusted open. She said, " Please, I need your help. Will you take my umbrella down so I can see the sunshine?"

What greater purpose does our life hold than to be an instrument of God's love to another? As an incest survivor, I believe one of my purposes in life is to help take down the rusted umbrellas of guilt and shame for those who are sitting under a cloud of darkness.

We are in many ways our brothers' and sisters' keepers, and I think as survivors of whatever our tragedy, we have an edge on how to effectively help another, for we have walked in their shoes, so to speak. Sandra Burdich, author of *Secrets of the Heart* challenges us to make our misery our ministry. Have you ever wondered what your purpose in life is? Sharing your experiences and the knowledge you've gained is important, for many are hungry for answers.

Once you start telling your story, others will come forth with theirs, which will be the starting point of their healing. It is very gratifying to be able to help another person begin their journey to wholeness. Our story and the information we share may be what another is waiting to hear.

I challenge each one to be intuitive toward the needs of others and ready to help those we meet. This doesn't require a lot of talent or a doctorate degree. Just be open and listen, and guide victims to people and resources that will help them. You could even hand them this book. Our genuine concern could be the *starting fluid* another needs to get them going on their journey to health and freedom.

An important event happened during my time of recovery that I have not yet shared. I found I gained a sensitivity that I didn't know I had until recently. I am able to cry with people when they share their heartaches with me. Before this time, I would listen compassionately, but for some reason, tears never came. As I mentioned earlier, while I was a child, I had to learn to silence my tears and cut off my emotions. Since then, it has been difficult to cry, especially in public, or to show my true emotions. But at last, it has finally happened.

I remember the first time I felt tears of compassion, and it took me by surprise. A friend was relating to me her story of how her daughter was sexually abused, and the horrible pain she experienced for her daughter. Tears began to fill my eyes as I listened. At first, I was a bit embarrassed, but then I became overjoyed, for I realized then they were tears from heaven. The novocaine had worn off my heart and I could feel her pain. My tears demonstrated to her just how much I really cared without my having to say a word. It was a tender and grateful moment.

On my journey, I also found that I also gained a *spirit of truth*. I was so sick of living with lies and telling them, that it was imperative—even a compulsive need—to be truthful in every word and thought that came into my mind. I found myself correcting even my slightest exaggeration. Exaggerating was a way of life, a bad habit that my siblings and I learned while we were growing up— and one that needed correcting. *The truth truly set me free, and in that freedom I found energy, creativity, and wisdom that was before unknown to me.*

Some parts of my healing took only a few months, and others took a few years. *The important fact is, healing did take place, and that's the most important part of my story.*

As I'm nearing my journey's end, I realize that in many ways, I have really only begun to learn about God, faith, and life. I am a work in progress. Somewhere along the way I've discovered I am a much stronger person than I ever realized. I also learned patience, for I was in a hurry to be healthy and to put the incest behind me. I can truthfully tell you that I have never been healthier, emotionally or physically, than now. My relationships with my husband and children have never been better, my faith more real, nor my courage stronger. These are wonderful years, and my prayer is that anyone who has experienced similar abuse will find the same peace and joy that I've found. It can happen.

One afternoon, my grandson Phillip asked, "Grandma, what's the worst thing that ever happened to you?" I was startled by his question and didn't know exactly how to answer him. Do I tell him about the incest? I finally came up with an acceptable answer even though it scooted around the truth a bit.

I said, "Holding in a terrible secret. But, when I finally told it, it became the best secret I ever told."

His next question was, "What was that secret, Grandma?"

I knew it was coming. I told him that when I was a girl, my father touched me in places he never should have, and that made me feel very bad.

He nodded his head as if he understood, and my answer satisfied him.

I have shared with you my life, including my worst secret. I've also shared it with many others. Telling has been a life changing experience, for with the telling, came healing, knowledge, love and restitution.

The other day my friend Tinker asked, "Now, Shirley, I heard you say we should make gain from our pain. So what are the things you gained from your painful experience?" I responded by telling her that I had gained much. My list is a long one. I hope I don't bore you.

I gained a spirit of truth, an authentic faith, and a vibrant marriage. I am slower to accommodate others on demand. I have learned not only to like myself, but also to love myself. I am not as vulnerable or naive. I have learned to have a healthy view of men. I readily speak of the needs of others, and don't avoid confrontations. I've developed self-confidence. I am a better wife, mother, friend, and listener. I'm a more sensitive nurse. I am a risk taker. I am wiser, and more educated. I'm a better composer and musician. I can feel emotions. I have developed skills that will help me through all of life's adversities, and I feel worthy to be loved and to give love freely in return. I gained my freedom!

Yes, I have gained much, yet new challenges continue to arise—new opportunities, I prefer to call them. It seems just when things are comfortable, up pops a new concern I need to deal with. At that moment, I start again with what has worked before and begin to put into practice all the lessons I have learned through my healing process. First, I share my concern with the One who has become my source of strength, the One who is working toward my good. Yes, my burden quickly transfers to God, and I stay open to His guidance. Then I quickly find a loved one to confide in, and also learn as much as I can about the new situation. Next, I make a beeline to my Yamaha keyboard, and before long, the magnitude of my problem has shrunk, or I've gained insight on how to best handle the situation. I have programmed myself to look beyond the difficulty, to have hope, and *not to worry*. That process has made my life so much easier. This solution lifts me above life's adversities and lets me experience a certain amount of peace, even in the midst of my problems.

As I reached out to God, my music compositions began to take on new depth and beauty. My new sense of peace and gratitude inspired me to title my first instrumental CD "Come With Me To A Place Called Peace". I named it after a verse in the Bible that became my motto: "Let the peace of God rule in your heart and refuse to worry about anything" (Colossians 3:15). My faith helped me to make peace with my past, and that peace has allowed me to put my burdens to rest.

Healing from sexual abuse is a process. I wish I could tell you there is one quick fix but there is not. Healing is like peeling an onion, ridding yourself of one stinky layer at a time until you get to the tender heart of the onion. And the ironic part of the stinky layers is; none of it was your doing, yet, the layers have to go or else you will continue to repel those around you leaving you isolated and lonely. I'm talking about stinky behaviors and attitudes, stinky ways of thinking and acting. They need to go. Change has to happen. I had no ideas how I offended people or how people thought of me. I was so plastic, phony, and shallow. It is no wonder I had few true friends. They wanted more only at that time, I didn't have more to give. You can't give what you don't have. I was a wounded, shameful victim of sexual abuse surviving the best I knew how, and I had built a barrier around me so I would never get hurt again.

As I examined the areas of my life where I experienced abuse (abandonment, emotional, verbal, sexual, and spiritual) I got closer and closer to the reality of how my abuse had affected me. I also began to realize that life doesn't revolve around me. My abuse made me self centered and I understand now why, because I was all I had to protect me. Thankfully, that is no longer the case. After I told my story, Jim and others were able to pour love on me and I felt their love, and with that love came, truth, protection and security. Their love convinced me of my worth and I began to feel worthy, valuable and confident. They were God with skin on to me and gave me a glimpse of what God's love must be like. They loved me whole.

The bottom line is, love is what heals. Until our wounds get the love and attention they need they continue to weep and bring us pain. Knowledge helps us understand the "why's" and "how's" but it is love that patches up our holes and turns us outward focused. The more I reach out and love on others and allow others to love on me my sexual abuse had less and less of an impact on my life. It is so important for victims to seek help, to get into a support group, to share their story with a trusted friend or counselor and let others love on them until they are well. They then need to spread that love on to others in what ever capacity they can for it is love that heals.

It was another one of those perfect, summer evenings in late July. The full moon shimmered beautifully across Lake Cadillac, as the gentle breeze flowed freely through our upstairs bedroom window. I was lying comfortably in our queen size bed, reflecting on all the enjoyable activities of the day, when I felt Jim roll over to my side of the bed as he had so many times before. He lovingly laid his right hand on my thigh and gently began to slide it up under my nightgown. You can be assured that this time I did not turn away from him like I had so many times before. The memory of my sexual abuse never entered my mind. I could experience and return Jim's love, completely unattached from my past. Now that is a miracle, and something I thought was worth sharing with others. Sexual abuse does not have to wreck your life. You can recover and be better than brand new!

"Thank You, Lord"

You're the beginning and the end,
You're the circle that I'm within.
You're the glory in each new day,
You calm my nights as I lay.

You're the peace within my soul,
And the contentment as I grow old.
You filled my life yet set me free
You made living Lord,
What it ought to be.

Jim and Shirley with daughters, 2004.

Part 2:
A Guide to Living Free

Twenty-eight practical steps to overcome sexual abuse

1. Commit to making your life the best possible, and doing what it takes to make it happen.
2. Have faith in a Higher Power and draw from that strength.
3. Think positively. Believe things will get better. Your heart will heal if you allow it.
4. If you haven't already; remove yourself from the abusive situation.
5. Tell your story, and share your pain. Healing begins by telling.
6. Seek support from family members, friends, counselors, and supports groups.
7. Develop a hobby or take a class. Focus on something other than your abuse.
8. Read, ask questions, and research your particular situation.
9. Make good nutrition, exercise, and rest part of your everyday regimen.
10. Develop an attitude of gratitude, and look for the good in life. It's there.
11. Make yourself accountable to another to keep you moving forward.
12. Pray, meditate, and soak in inspirational material daily.
13. Adopt mercy as a way of life. Forgive others—and yourself.
14. Visualize the life you dream of having, and set goals to achieve it.

15. Reach out, volunteer, help others, and share your story. Others need encouragement.
16. Take advantage of the benefits in music and humor. They are great natural uppers.
17. Refuse pity parties and eliminate that "the world owes me" attitude. Avoid negative thinking and negative people; likewise, seek out positive people.
18. Confront your abuser, for we can't conquer what we won't confront. If not possible, write a letter—even if he or she is deceased.
19. If recommended by your doctor, use medications, but understand that mood enhancers are a crutch, not a cure.
20. Journal your thoughts. Write your own book.
21. Have patience with yourself—and others. Healing takes time.
22. Protect yourself by setting boundaries. Put protective barriers around your heart, and distance yourself from those who weaken you.
23. Love yourself. Think of yourself as a person of worth. God thinks so, and so do I.
24. Feed yourself affirmations. "I will conquer this." "I am not wrecked for life, only wiser than most." "I will not allow my past to ruin my future."
25. Realize you can only change yourself, and accept the things you cannot change.
26. Look people in the eye. Walk tall. Every day is a new beginning, and a chance to grow and heal.
27. Smile, and the world will smile with you.
28. Hug a lot. Embrace life, for it can be very sweet!

*I*f you have already read my story, these steps probably sound familiar to you, for they were interwoven into the story. When I started my journey, I did not have a particular list to follow. As I found a resource that was beneficial, I put it in my memory bank. I finally ended up with a list that ultimately became an important map, one that led me to my destination to find health and peace. What I have presented on the following pages is additional information intended to make the map easier for others to read as they journey on to find wholeness for themselves. As simple and basic as some of these helps are, it is important to be reminded of their benefits, especially during difficult times.

You may be at the crossroads, where you are deciding to take the first step and face the situation in your life that has greatly injured you. I hope you choose to move forward and create the life you have always dreamed of having. *Have faith in yourself.* That's extremely important. A force greater than yourself will point you in the right direction, but you have to be willing to follow that voice. We are designed with abilities waiting to burst forth in times of need, but we will never know until we dare to release our fears and begin.

Is faith really necessary?

While working in the hospital, I heard physicians often remark that their patients who had a faith did much better than those who did not. I found that also to be true in my home-health nursing career. Having a faith and drawing from that power is very beneficial. That is why I encourage everyone to whole-heartedly embrace a faith.

By now you have learned that my faith is in Christ Jesus. I am a Christian. My childhood environment nurtured my yearning for a meaningful faith. It was breathed and fed to me since birth. However, it never completely made sense because of my father's double standards. I saw wrongs and inconsistencies that led me to question my faith. That is why my search to find the truth about *the God of my youth* was so important.

All I have said regarding the God in which I believe might sound confusing or even strange to one who has no profession of faith—or who believes in a different religion. That's understandable. I hope you will be patient while I explain further why Christianity works for me.

During my study, I became convinced, like millions before me, that there is a higher power that orchestrated our existence. I also believe like many, that our spirit is immortal.

Christianity recognizes God, Jesus, and The Holy Spirit, all rolled up into one, as the highest power. Many Bible scholars call the *three in one* the "Holy Trinity", however that phrase is not in the Bible. Christianity also believes there is a spirit that works against God and his principles, and the Bible calls that evil spirit Satan.

The spirit of evil is not only seen in the events on the nightly news stations; we all struggle from time to time with thoughts and deeds that aren't pure. I believe the goal of Satan is to separate us from our loving God and his redeeming ways.   When we nurture feelings of hate, revenge, selfishness, etc, we have allowed the evil force to win. Our negative reactions to what others have done to us can destroy our spirit, our health, our relationships, and our peace. That is why I try to do anything I can to stop evil powers from influencing my life and stealing my happiness. One way I do this is to mentally and verbally dismiss it! I tell it to leave this place and me. The Bible tells us that the spirit of evil is very powerful, but God gave us power to overcome the evil spirit. Thus, I can prevent it from influencing me and destroying my happiness by removing its presence from my life. I use this practice every time I feel the presence of evil and it works.

It is so important for me to think positively about life, people, and to work toward what is good and right. As a child of God, I believe I was created to walk in love and light, and not to allow anything to dampen that spirit in me. My belief and confidence in Almighty God, my loving Higher Power has given me the strength to stay focused on that goal.

I believe tapping into a *power higher* than ourselves is ultimately the most important thing we can do. This may be an awkward step for some; however, I feel it is one we all need to take, for the rewards are tremendous.

When we take the step of faith and surrender to a higher power, we have given ourselves an incredible gift, the gift of hope. As this happens, despair begins to leave, making room for optimism and eventually a new attitude develops. In the Bible, the book of Ezekiel, chapter 36:27, are these words: "I will give you a new heart and put a new spirit in you." That's encouraging.

You may have already noticed that relying on a higher power is important in Twelve-Step recovery programs. Many of our problems are just too big for us to solve by ourselves *and were never intended to be handled alone. We need divine inspiration and intervention.*

Faith in a higher power starts with acknowledging the power and grace of God. We realize we need help, so we venture to go beyond what our eyes can see and choose to believe. That higher power has a name, and for me, it's Almighty God.

Once we have said the important words, "I believe," we need to trust in God and believe we will receive help. Believe that somehow, some way, God will make good come out of your life and give you peace. I believe the God in the Bible is very real and wants to help us. The Bible tells us that we were created with a spirit that is made to last forever, and God hopes we will choose to spend eternity with Him, because he loves us. God doesn't need our love or us, for He is self-sustaining. Yet, He gave us the gift of life so we could enjoy all the wonders He created as well as have a loving relationship with us. Most importantly, God came down in the form of Jesus with a mission to *forgive* and *heal* us, and I find that very amazing and humbling.

I recently came across Rick Warren's book *The Purpose Driven Life.* In it, he explains what happens when we choose to believe. He says once we *believe, we belong* to the family of God and have available to us all the benefits and privileges of being in His family. Warren goes further to say that everyone was created by God, but not everyone is a child of God (Galatians 3:26). That has to be our choice. Once we choose to be a part of God's family, God says we are born again into His family. Rick Warren's book has a wealth of information about God and His plan for our lives. It's a helpful resource for believers or inquirers of the Christian faith alike.

One friend told me that she just didn't have it. She said that she didn't have any faith at all. My answer to her was, "Who does, at first?" Our faith and relationship with God is something to be developed, much like one with a friend or spouse. The more we talk about God with others and study for ourselves, the deeper our understanding of God will become. In the Bible, it says that faith comes by hearing. (Romans 10:17) The more we put into it, the greater our faith will be. Faith in God is a positive leap that takes us into the light. It is a decision, not necessarily a feeling.

Even when I doubted the existence of God, He did not abandon me. He loved me still and helped me to find the truth. I've learned that God can handle our doubts, and encourages us to search for answers, for when we do, God is more likely to be found.

If you are yearning for a meaningful faith, I recommend you start reading and search for the truth yourself. Also, pray for inspiration. Talk about God with other positive people of faith. I'm convinced you *will* find a wonderful, powerful faith and a lasting peace. Seek and you will find!

Make positive thinking a lifelong habit.

Webster defines positive as "expressing affirmation, very confident, absolute certain, not negative."

We need to train ourselves to think positive about every aspect of our life. Remembering to look for the *good* in life needs to become a habit. And how do we do that?

One thing that helped me to stay on a positive track was to put positive messages around where I would read them often. My favorite spot was in the bathroom. One friend sticks her favorite quotes into her wallet, another puts them in her makeup bag.

The words we say and thoughts that we feed ourselves are important, for we believe and become what we say and think we are.

It is equally important to never feed ourselves downer, negative words. They are poison to our spirit. Refuse to let evil drag you down, and never tell yourself that you can't, or it won't happen, or you are doomed. Dismiss those thoughts immediately and replace them with positive words that give you hope, such as:

"I am a person of worth."

"I will not let my past ruin my future."

"I will not believe the lies told to me."

"I refuse to be victimized any further."

"Tomorrow will be better."

"I am a survivor."

"I will get past this!"

"I am not wrecked for life, just wiser than most."

"I will conquer this."

"I am a child of God and not alone in this."

An important statement I often repeat to myself is: "Let it go!"

Nurture your soul with affirmations often. They are wonderful nutrients that help to build strong healthy minds and bodies. We should *love ourselves*, and one way to do that is to give self-affirmations. You are worthy and loved by God regardless of your past or present circumstance.

Norman Vincent Peale, the author of *The Power of Positive Thinking,* believes that what we think; we will become, good or bad, strong or weak, victorious or defeated, so we need to practice being a positive thinker.

I agree with author and speaker Charles Swindoll when he says that life is 10% what happens to us and 90% how we react to it.

Our attitude about our situation is the most important element that controls our happiness. You need to believe you will recover and overcome, believe you are innocent, believe you are worthy of love, respect and a good life, and believe you are forgiven. Have hope, for healing is possible! One man in our support group refused to believe he could ever be any differently. He was convinced he was doomed forever to suffer from the consequences from his abuse. When I told him differently he left for he did not believe life could be different. I can tell you this because it happened to me. Healing is possible. Don't accept less. God does not love me any more than he does you. He wants healing for you too. He wants healing for your perpetrator.

How many times have you heard that attitude is everything? Well, add "positive" to the word "attitude", and you have given yourself power to overcome seemingly insurmountable situations. Make it a habit to find something positive about everything. It is there. We just have to be creative and find it. We should also give positive strokes to those around us. It's great fertilizer for their emotional health. Learning to fill each day with positive thoughts as well as speaking them out loud is a great tool to help overcome depression. *Ask others to correct you when you talk negatively.* Think positively and be confident that things will get better, and they most likely will.

One of the most positive preachers of today is Robert Schuller. He has written many inspirational books, and the common theme in them is the importance of having a positive attitude. I originally became acquainted with Dr Schuller through his TV ministry. His "power thoughts" were the words that inspired me to be a positive thinker, and I still read them nearly every day. Through Dr. Schuller's teachings, I learned that Jesus was the most positive person in the world, and He wants us to follow His example.

God has placed inside each one of us abilities that will help us conquer difficult situations, and thinking positively is an important one.

Some of Schuller's favorite "power thoughts", from his book of the same title, have also become mine:

Tough times never last. Tough people do.

Never let a problem become an excuse.

Capitalize on your pain!

Never allow a fractured experience to shape your future.

His books are sold widely, and I recommend them for interesting reading and great counsel.

To help us stay on a positive course, we need to avoid negative influences, whether they are negative friends or family members, movies or reading materials, news stations, or television shows. Refuse to be in situations that will drag you down and produce negative feelings. We need to put a protective hedge around ourselves, and refuse to let anything sift through that isn't uplifting and good, *especially when we are emotionally fragile.* We also need to set boundaries and not allow others to compromise our standards or our goals. This could be a good time to break away from old friends and habits that hold us back. If you are unsure on how to set boundaries or keep them, read the book *Boundaries* by Townsend and Cloud.

I have found Philippians 4:8 to be an excellent guide to follow. It states, *"Whatever is true, whatever is noble, whatever is right, whatever is pure, whatever is lovely, whatever is admirable, if anything is excellent or praiseworthy, think about these things."*

Opening the window of your Soul

I've been told that what makes human beings special from other creatures is that we have the ability to communicate on a level that is higher than that of other creatures. I also believe we are given that ability because we are human, emotional beings, and need to relate at that level to survive and to be happy. I've mentioned many times the importance of communicating your emotional pain to another. It is the very first step toward finding healing. We need to communicate what is troubling us in some way to another. By communication, pain can be alleviated, knowledge can be gained, and help can be given. It is crucial that we continue to talk until we find relief from our pain, for telling is transforming. In the situation of incest or sexual abuse, we need to get past the shame and start talking.

Likewise, communication is also critical to the success of any personal relationship. We should always keep up on skills that will help us improve our relationships. Bad communication can become our worst enemy, for the mixed signals we receive can divide and devastate relationships. Sometimes when we think we know what the other person is saying, it is helpful to relate it back to them. This often clarifies misunderstandings before they can become larger.

Communicating with God, I believe, is the most powerful connection we can make. God does not limit communication to just words. Connecting with our Heavenly Father can happen in many different ways, such as through music, awesome surroundings, through prayer, inspired written words, while performing acts of love, and through other people. His presence and love can be known to anyone, anywhere, at anytime. We only need to recognize it is God speaking to us and tune Him in.

Prayer is just another word for talking or communicating with God. It's our pipeline to God, and it is to our benefit that we make it an automatic part of our lives. Prayer seemed awkward and difficult until I made it a habit of thinking my prayers to God throughout my day, no matter what I was doing.

I drive a fair distance to work, so I take the opportunity to talk to God about anything I choose during that time. I thank Him for my many blessings, and applaud Him for the beautiful sunrise that's before me. I ask Him for guidance on decisions, and ask Him to help my children and to keep them close to Him. I also ask for ideas on what I should plan for supper. That may sound trivial, but to me, it's important, for at the end of the day, I'm brain dead—with no ideas. I also need periods of silence to listen to God's voice within. That is why it is important to find a quiet, undistracted place where I can concentrate on God and be receptive to whatever thoughts He'd like to put in my head. Jim gets weary of my small talk, but I think God likes it, for I never feel cut off from Him. I'm more likely to cut God short by my business or lack of concentration.

We need to communicate as if we have our best friend right beside us, because we do. The Bible says,

"When we draw close to God, God will draw close to us." (James 4:8).

It is an awesome privilege to be able to talk to the God of the universe and know that He truly loves us and cares about every aspect of our lives. I believe that's His main *trumpet call* to the world! When we truly believe this, and realize the *Most High* is on our side, even the darkest situation becomes hopeful. That important revelation can lift and empower us to face any challenge.

Even if you do not claim to be a person of faith, I recommend that you start thinking about God. You have nothing to lose. If you feel awkward about praying, just humble yourself and say what is in your heart. God will be there with you.

A simple prayer such as, "Jesus, I accept you as my savior and I want you in my life," is a great beginning. I am wordier so mine went more like the following,

> "Almighty God, I want to believe in you. I am choosing to believe in you and in your son Jesus. However, because of my abuse, the "Holy Good Father image" is difficult to identify with, and I struggle coming to you. I also have many unanswered question. Yet, I yearn to believe in you, and want to love you. I am accepting that you love me, and came to earth in Jesus to show me just how much. You died a horrible death.
>
> Please forgive my sins and help me to forgive others. I have a lot of baggage. Help me unload it, and to be free from the burdens it has caused me. Help me to stay true to you for I am weak. I want to grow and know you better. God, Thank-you for adopting me as your child. I am honored and so thankful. I look forward to our new relationship with much anticipation.

God hears our prayers and when he sees a repentant heart he offers us a *heavens helping* of mercy and grace. God loves us so deeply we can't comprehend it. God came to earth in the form of Jesus to save us not to criticize or condemn us. We have a loving caring God that wants to be our companion, to bless us and heal us.

The reason I emphasize how much God loves us is that it took me a long time to really get that message. I needed to experience it, and to hear and read about God's love over and over before I could understand and believe it was true.

When we tell our story it allows others the opportunity to love us as God would if he were sitting right beside us. We victims need an abundance of love and assurance. Love is the ingredient that rebuilds self-confidence, and removes shame. Whereas, confession and repentance of our sins makes us feel worthy to receive love.

I've learned that neither shame, nor the sins I've committed, has any effect on my ability to approach God. He loves me as I am yet he is there to empower me to do better, and overcome the problems that were created because of my abuse.

I also finally realized that my father's sins blackened him, not me. For years, I was carrying around displaced shame. The shame from the incest belongs solely to my father, and was not for me to bear. That realization helped to release my shame. To God, I was a beautiful child of His, and He was glad I finally came to Him. The Bible says that all heaven rejoices when one soul comes to our Heavenly Father.

We are never too dirty or sinful to approach the Most High. Nor, do we have to work and do good deeds to earn that privilege. God's Grace is for all people and covers all sins. I find that incredibly amazing!

Strengthening the inner self

There is much said about being alone and getting in touch with our own inner self to gain strength and balance for the challenges in life. But what happens when our inner-self is hollow and our self-worth is that of a doormat? Getting in touch with our inner self is not an easy task for victims of abuse, for we see little value in ourselves. We question every decision we make and our own abilities. We have been made to feel like we are nothing, so why would we like to be around ourselves or think others would either?

In a child psychology class, I learned that we begin in infancy to develop our sense of self-worth. It is reflected back to us in the eyes of those closest to us. If our caregivers reflect back to us a sense of worthlessness, then that is how we portray ourselves. So where do we begin to retrieve our self-worth if we have no sense of value?

While in school, the praise from teachers and coaches helped a great deal. In my early-married years, I found that I gained a certain amount of self-worth in caring for my family and doing good deeds for others. The praise I received and the "warm fuzzies" began to fill my empty inner space. Unfortunately, I became driven to do even more and more. Consequently, I found myself exhausted from doing too many good deeds. That was not healthy, either. I did not know how to set boundaries for myself; consequently, I couldn't say "no" to requests. My emotional balance was off.

Many use meditation techniques and yoga as ways to get in touch with their inner self. Those activities only seemed to fill my time, not my inner space. However, being still in beautiful surroundings and majestic settings (like the Grand Canyon) helped me to grasp the big picture of life and reminded me that someone mighty is in charge.

Jim and I were delighted when we were able to buy our modest house on Lake Cadillac twenty years ago, for it was always one of our dreams to be able to live on a lake. I had no idea how blessed I would be by that experience. My home has become my sanctuary, as I look out our living room window and gaze at my beautiful surroundings. Just fifty feet in front of me is a relaxing scene of mallards and herons swimming and diving for food in the bluish gold water. Gentle wooded hills line the south shore. The sunrises and sunsets are as equally breathtaking as any I've seen, as the radiant hues of orange and pink reflect like a mirror on the still lake. It is comforting when I stop for a moment to look through our sliding glass door and view what is before me, and to remember just who created all this, and who is in control. In my silence, I allow myself to be connected with my creator, and somehow that gives me a wonderful sense of peace and well-being. What my eyes behold is a reminder that the God of the universe, the one who created the sun that shines in my window, is also in me, in the form of His Holy Spirit. And He is willing to help me throughout my day. I am part of His family, and that makes me feel special and thankful.

If your "home sweet home" happens to be a one-room suite in a busy city, peek out the window, linger as you look up, and absorb the wonder and beauty there. Taking time to soak in the simple pleasures of life and focusing on the blessings that are there for us is a wonderful way to refresh our inner selves. We take so much for granted. Those bounties, which are free, offer so much.

Knowledge is for the taking, however wisdom comes from a greater source

Being able to read, or process what we read, takes a healthy mind. When I first began to talk about the incest, I fell into a great depression, and even reading was difficult for a time. That is why I was drawn to music for solace. I learned my reading problem was a common one during the recovery process. When I could concentrate on reading again, I couldn't get enough, and I searched for anything that might be helpful.

I have compiled a list of books on the bibliography page, ones I have read that were helpful. They are good for anyone who would like more information regarding sexual abuse as well as for those who need relief from it.

In my search for more understanding, I attempted again to read the Bible. For years after the abuse, I seldom read it, for all it brought was a disturbing voice from the past. The promises I once read seemed empty, and the stories fake. But that has changed. As I read, I came across stories and verses in the Bible that were comforting, some I never remembered reading before. Since that time, much of the Bible has become a true source of inspiration. I would like to share with you a few of my favorite verses in the Bible that have brought me great comfort. They are from the NIV version of the Bible.

"Who shall separate us from the love of Christ? Shall tribulation, or distress, or persecution, or fatigue, or *nakedness*, or peril, or sword? In all these things we are more than conquerors through Him who loved us." Romans 8:35-37

"God has not given us a spirit of fear, but of power and of love and of a sound mind." II Timothy 1:7

"The Lord is the strength of my life, of whom shall I be afraid?" Psalms 27:18

"Put on the *new you* who is renewed in knowledge according to the image of God who created you." Colossians 3:10

"Always pursue what is good both for yourselves and for all." II Thessalonians 5:15

"The truth will set you free." St John 8:32

"The Lord is my rock and my fortress and my deliverer." Psalms 18:2

"One thing I do, forgetting those things which are behind and reaching forward to those things which are ahead." Philippians 3:13

"For God is not the author of confusion but of peace." 1st Corinthians 14:33

"I will instruct you and teach you in the way which you should go; I will counsel you and keep my eyes upon you." Psalms 32:8

"Choose for yourself this day whom you will serve, but for me and my house, we will serve the Lord." Joshua 24:15

"You have turned my mourning into dancing... clothed me with gladness...

O Lord, my God, I will give you thanks to you forever." Psalms 30:11,12

"Bless the Lord and forget not all His benefits: Who forgives, *heals*, redeems, crowns, satisfies, so that your youth is renewed like the eagle's." Psalms 103:1-5

Those ancient yet inspiring words have power to comfort even today. All I have written seems inferior to what God has inspired others to write. Yet, I know what I have written is important, for God has inspired me to write as well. I prayed for God's guidance as I wrote every page. I know God inspires individuals today, just as He did the women and men in biblical times, and when He does, I believe it is our responsibility to share what we have learned so others may also benefit.

Maybe I have encouraged you to read the Bible and search for special verses that will comfort you. I hope I have. They will be a source of encouragement to you as you continue on your journey, as well as for a lifetime.

If you have never read the Bible before, I recommend you start with the New Testament and get an updated version of the Bible. A Bible commentator is also very helpful. It helps to explain what you are reading. I especially enjoyed reading The Message Bible, The Living Bible, and NIV translation of the Bible.

Forgiving the impossible sins

Certain crimes against humanity seem beyond forgiving. I think we each have our own opinion on what those crimes are. I considered the betrayal of my father one of them. It took me years before I was convinced that forgiving my father was a necessary step in my healing. When I began to understand what forgiveness was and why it is important, I finally allowed that process to begin in my heart.

As I searched for information on forgiving, I was surprised to see how much material is written on the subject of forgiveness. There are volumes out there, secular and religious, and their purpose is to assist others as they learn the seemingly forgotten art of forgiving.

Studies have shown that our willful act of forgiving is in correlation to our emotional and physical health. The act of showing mercy toward those who has injured us is a sacrificial deed that benefits us. Books on forgiveness are also included on the bibliography page.

For information on what the Bible says about forgiveness, you may want to start by reading Matthew

6:14, Matthew18: 35, and Luke 6:37. In those verses, I found it very interesting that God forgives my transgressions in the same proportion in which I forgive those who sin against me. My confession and repenting are necessary, but I must also put in place this next vital step, for I, too, am in need of forgiveness. Forgiving others is an important part of becoming free. Likewise, holding grudges and hanging on to past hurts only depletes our energy, and keeps us tied to the past—ruining our chances for happiness.

As I said earlier, God's ways often seem unnatural and difficult to us humans. Yet, because God is all knowing and certainly wiser than I, what better source can I go to for truth and inspiration, especially on matters of the heart?

The sins I committed to facilitate my escape from the incest troubled me deeply until I finally asked God to forgive me. For years, I tried to justify what I did as means of survival, and refused to accept any responsibility for my actions. Many people agreed with me and told me to let that part go, but their comments never took my guilt away. A heavy load was lifted when I finally confessed my sins and asked God for forgiveness. I needed to confess them for my peace of mind. I felt terrible for what I'd done, no matter what the circumstance was. It was extremely freeing to experience God's forgiveness. God's gift of *Grace* is a marvelous gift.

I want to clarify once again that forgiving is not saying the wrong committed against us was OK, or excusing it. Not at all. Sexual abuse is a very evil sin. Forgiveness sets the victim free. We repeat in the Lords Prayer, "Forgive us our sins as we forgive those who sin against us." For Christians, forgiving is an act of obedience.

"I forgive you" is a powerful verbal statement to the one who abused us that lets them know we are willing to let the situation go permanently. There may still be legal ramifications for their crimes that need to be paid, however the issue of forgiveness between the two is resolved, and that is very important for both concerned.

I also learned that forgiveness does not always lead to reconciliation, or a full restoration of the earlier relationship. Many things determine that factor, safety, for one. There are consequences to sins, and the scars on the victims reveal that. Healing in broken relationships may come but it could take years; as long as it takes for the victims to heal, and for perpetrators to be rehabilitated. One must feel completely safe around their abuser before a relationship can be reestablished.

Consequently, we shouldn't feel guilty for not wanting to be around our perpetrator, nor should we be forced to be with them until we feel comfortable. For many, restoration may never happen here on this earth.

I forgave my father, but I always insisted on having someone around me when I was with him. I did not feel safe around him even when he was 70, for he was not emotionally healthy. He was a psychopath. All sex offenders who prey upon children are, and they should not be trusted until a doctor tells you otherwise. I did not fear my father because of possible further sexual abuse, but for the emotional abuse that could occur. His controlling influence was powerful, and I needed to space myself until I was strong enough to handle it. When the story came out, I avoided my father intentionally for a time. I broke from him and his control. I needed space and time to gain strength and wisdom. My behavior may have seemed to others as if I did not forgive my father, but that was not the case. Those who have experienced the gravity of sexual abuse certainly understand the power our perpetrator can have over us. Forgiving another frees our spirit. However, forgiving our perpetrator does not guarantee our protection from further harm. That is why we should always have someone with us whenever we choose to be around our abuser.

Finding your creative edge

I have always enjoyed all kinds of artwork, from sculptures to paintings. In high school, I majored in art and hoped one day to become an art teacher. My sister Naomi reminded me how dramatic my painting became once I was married and away from my father. I would paint sunsets and sunrises in rich, vivid colors that mirrored the beautiful new life I was experiencing. Through the years, I found different media of art and craftwork to be very enjoyable. Somehow the use of acrylics or oils, or working with wet clay and molding it into something lovely, made me feel lovely also. The time I took creating gave my mind a break, and the activity became a great stress reliever.

If you have never tried working with art forms before, visit your local art store. There are many art media to choose from. One may intrigue you enough to try. Some of the best artwork ever done was created in times of extreme distress or great joy. Who knows? You may find a hidden talent and be the next Norman Rockwell or Michelangelo, so dig in, and don't be afraid to get your hands dirty.

Art can be also be found in wood working, working with clay, needle point, photography, flower arranging or gardening. The important message here is to allow art to be an important break from your story, and allow it to bless you.

Time to Set Boundaries

Everyone needs to construct healthy emotional boundaries. Boundaries keep us safe. They tell our limits and are guidelines to others who want to be in our life. Our boundaries tell a lot about us; what we will take and not take, what we allow or not allow, what we stand for and what is important to us, what kind of people we want in our life and those we want out. Think about the boundaries you need to put in place. What do you want your life to be like?

Our boundaries need to be verbalized so others know where we stand and what our limits are. Our values and desires are not to be pushed aside. Your voice needs to be heard and obeyed. You have a right to set your own boundaries and to have others respect them. People will try to push your boundaries but a healthy person will stand firm and not allow harm to enter. Victims especially need to learn the importance of setting boundaries for most victims are clueless about boundaries. We were never given boundaries, nor protected. We didn't even know they existed. Our boundaries were never built consequently; we continue to live in survival mode taking whatever is thrown at us. We don't realize we matter, nor have rights or power to set our boundaries.

In the book "Boundaries" by Dr. John Townsend, he explains the process of building healthy boundaries. The book illustrates well how life is with boundaries and the problems that often occur because of no boundaries. More importantly, it helps one to establish safe boundaries so victims can protect themselves from further harm. I recommend everyone reading "Boundaries".

Sources for help on the Web

I hope you take time to visit the following websites. They have valuable information and resources for victims of incest and sexual abuse.

SIA, Survivors of Incest Anonymous, at
www.siawso.org/
RAINN, Rape Abuse Incest National Network
www.rainn. org/
National Association to Protect Children
www.protect.org/
Assisting survivors of clergy abuse
www.thelinkup.org
www.openheartsministry.org
www.TroubledWith.com
Michigan Coalition Against Domestic and
Sexual Violence www.mcadsv.org
www.healingprivatewounds.org

Some of their statistical information may alarm you. I recommend going right to their sites. If you pull up other words, such as "incest", you will find ugly pornography advertisements that are extremely upsetting—just thought I should warn you.

There is also a toll-free national domestic violence hotline, 1-800-799-7233, which has a friendly representative ready to assist anyone. For deaf individuals, the number is 1 800-787-3224. The National Sexual Abuse Hotline is 1-800-656-HOPE (4673). The national child abuse hotline is 1 800 422 4453.

The people minding the phones are eager and waiting to be of service. You can call these numbers anytime, day or night.

To medicate – or not

friend of mine asked me what medications I took to help me through my time of depression. She was looking for some relief for herself. She was stunned when I told her that I never took any anti-depressants. The ironic thing about that is, I never thought to ask, nor did my doctor suggest them to me. If he did, I don't remember it. It was not that I was a super strong person; I was just so *out of it* that it never crossed my mind to ask. However, I know medications work, and for a time, they can be an important part of one's recovery. They are especially helpful for people who do not have a lot of support. The positive side of not taking medication is that I learned different ways to deal with depression that were effective. I believe the large amount of support I received from my family during that time also helped to alleviate the need for drugs.

Being a nurse has helped me be aware of the benefits of today's medications as well as their side effects. Each person's situation is unique, and the taking of medications may be beneficial to you for a period of time; in fact, they may even be life saving. A good friend reminded me how very important her medication was in her recovery process. Her depression was so great, she became suicidal. Her medication bought her time, and was the bridge that allowed her to feel somewhat healthy until she really was. To her it was lifesaving. There should not be any stigma for taking any medication your doctor prescribes, for they could benefit you greatly.

If you use medications, it is important for you and your loved ones to be aware of the side effects. One woman I knew took an anti-depressant, and it helped her depression until she gained 40 pounds. Then her weight gain depressed her even more.

I also recommend letting others, a spouse or trusted friend, administer the medications to you. In our delicate state of mind, it is easy for us to forget whether we have taken the medicines, and we can easily overdose ourselves by thinking just one more might help us even more. I have taken care of patients in the hospital who have done just that. They were brought into the emergency room and thought to have been possible suicide patients. In reality, they had only accidentally taken an overdose of their own medication. The concern I have with taking mood enhancing medications is that they merely help us to live with the problem. We need to learn to fix our problems permanently.

If you end up taking medication, you need not feel guilty about it. Just be sure to administer it wisely, and plan on getting off it eventually. There are many different drugs available. I could list them, but they would become outdated very soon. Your doctor will know which one is best for you, and make sure to be well informed about *all* the medications you take.

The best medicine in the world, however, is love. It can heal a multitude of wounds that afflict the spirit. By opening up and sharing my pain, it allowed others to shower love upon me. I was bathed in love by my husband, daughters, family members, close friends, and by my counselor. They heard me, consoled and comforted, and helped me to move forward. Their love restored my self-worth, and eventually closed the wounds in my heart. My loved ones were God in action, loving me like He does, for after all, love comes from God, and it's the best medicine of all.

How nutrition and exercise play roles in healing.

Medical doctor and surgeon Lorraine Day shares an interesting concept in her book *Cancer Doesn't Scare Me Anymore*. She believes that nearly all illnesses are caused by stress, dehydration, or malnutrition. She's convinced we give ourselves our diseases one day at a time by not getting enough water, nutrition, exercise, and by holding grudges and having an unforgiving spirit. She found that when we forgive, our cell structure changes, and that stress and unforgiveness suppress our immune systems.

In this segment, I am reinforcing the claims of many who state how important it is to get ample water and nutritious foods into our bodies. We hear reports on the benefit of good nutrition and exercise nearly every day, and hopefully most of you adhere to that advice. However, doing what's best does not always happen when we are under stress.

Depression drained my energy to where I didn't even want to think, let alone cook. I would grab anything handy such as cereal or sweets rather than prepare a healthy meal. It is important to know what foods are best for us, especially when we are under stress. Fresh fruits, vegetables—especially the dark green varieties—and whole grain breads are loaded with many of the important B vitamins, which help our bodies to produce hormones that help us handle stress. They also give us endurance, so reach for those foods first. A reminder; we need *at least* five servings of fruits or veggies a day. Many small nutritious meals keep our blood sugar stable and provide constant nutrition to our bodies. I recommend taking a good multivitamin every day to supplement your diet; to be sure you are getting the nutrients you need. Tri Vita B12 is a good sublingual vitamin. It melts under your tongue and is especially great if you have a hard time swallowing pills. Remembering to take the vitamins may be difficult, so put them in plain sight or in with your toothbrush so you will remember to take them. Those daily reminder pillboxes are also helpful.

I was encouraged to watch my caffeine and refined sugar intake so I could sleep better. I was also encouraged to drink lots of water. Depriving our body of the much-needed fluids inhibits proper body functions and slows down healing. Having bottles of purified water in your refrigerator helps to alleviate this problem, yet again, we need to remember to drink them. Most recommend eight 8oz. glasses of water a day; however; Doctor Day recommends 10 cups a day *on top* of the other beverages we normally drink.

Depression can also lead to overeating and weight gain. That is another reason to have healthy low-carb foods readily available. I have used delicious foods as a distraction from my pain many times. They helped to soothe my aching heart, entertained me, as well as gave me some degree of pleasure, for I love foods, especially creamy, cool delights. I now try to replace the high sugar foods with nuts, sunflower seeds, dried fruits, crispy bacon and sliced lean meats, yogurt, and cottage cheese along with plenty of raw fruits and vegetables. You will still see me with my share of goodies, but they are a treat—not a staple.

One way to love yourself is to feed your body nutritious foods. Our health is our responsibility, and it is important to make healthy eating choices.

Exercising and good nutrition are truly an important combination. I'm sure you've heard many times that exercising also alleviates stress. Studies have proven it does. Just getting outside and breathing in the fresh air is excellent for us. It regenerates our cells and helps us to release toxins from our body. I was given a set of headsets, and I've found they provide great entertainment as I walk, for I am not one who enjoys walking alone. Now that I have a cell phone, I visit with my daughters while I walk. Whatever it takes, just get out there and start moving. Body movement is vital for good body functions, so make a promise to yourself, and start doing something that keeps the ol' body moving.

Humor me!

A grandmother was surprised by her seven-year-old grandson one morning. He had made her coffee. She drank what was the worst cup of coffee in her life. When she got to the bottom, to her surprise were three of those little green army men in her cup. When she asked what they were doing in her cup her grandson answered, "Grandma, it says on the TV, "The best part of waking up is soldiers in your cup!"

A nursery school teacher was delivering a station wagon full of kids home one day when a fire truck zoomed past. Sitting in the front seat of the fire truck was a Dalmatian dog. The children started discussing the dog's duties. "They use him to keep crowds back," said one youngster. "No," said another, "He's just for good luck." A third child brought the argument to a close: "They use the dog," she said firmly, "to find the fire hydrant."

When my grandson asked me how old I was, I teasingly replied, "I'm not sure." "Look in your underwear, Grandma," he advised. "Mine says I'm four."

So much has been said about the benefits of good humor that I feel I need only to echo their claims. Everyone needs at least three good belly laughs a day—at least that's what my doctor told me. Humor is another natural amenity that elevates the production of our mood enhancing hormones. Researchers have recently learned that humor not only relaxes our blood vessels, but also widens them. Humor also stops the production of stress hormones.

We can find great humor in just about everything if we look for it. It's in books, comedies, videos and movies, animals, children, jokes, and my favorite, people-watching. I also like to watch those silly sit-coms, for they crack me up and make me laugh out loud. Look for the humor that surrounds you, and when you do find something that tickles you, don't hold back or feel embarrassed. Laugh freely! It's wonderful medicine for the heart.

I have two very special women friends, and when we become a threesome, it is inevitable that no matter what we do, we end up having a laughing good time. To others, it may look silly to see three grown women having so much fun and making so much noise. We enjoy each other's company so much that we don't even care. After I return home, I realize just how good that laughter is, for that energy from laughing lasts for hours. I also realize how lucky I am to have those two dear friends in my life.

Seek out people who make you laugh and feel good. Their positive attitude and light spirit can become wonderfully contagious. Laughter and good humor are wonderful gifts to us.

Another positive feature about humor is it puts a smile on our face, a genuine one.

For years I smiled so others would not see my pain. Put on a happy face regardless, that's what my mother did. I didn't realize that my constant smiling turned others off until a true friend told me so. My smiles may have covered up my pain, but they also made me seem phony. Yet, all of me was not phony, only part; but only I could decipher what part was real and what wasn't. As I grew, my smiles continued, but they became authentic. There is a genuine quality in them that wasn't there before, and others have noticed the difference. I am sincerely a happy person, and as I smile, I have noticed that the world smiles back, and that makes me feel great. A smile is a great gift to give away as well as to receive, especially if they are for real.

To stay on course we need a coach

To help you stay on course, it is important you have someone you trust that you will be accountable to, one you will listen to and take instructions from. Choose someone with whom you feel comfortable sharing your highs and lows, and your progress as well as your regressions. We need someone from whom we can take correction. In fact, we need to tell them to correct us when we slip back into old habits. There were times when I needed my husband to remind me to get back on track. His correction was very helpful. We need to be reminded when we are going down the wrong path. Soon you will be telling yourself, "No. I'm not going to go there."

I love to watch the beautiful cloud formations in the sky. I think that started when I was a child. I remember lying in the grass and looking up at the heavens while I tried to make images out of the amazing, different shaped clouds. Even today, I enjoy doing it. I try to visualize God's image up in the clouds. Often, I can see His gentle face or hand reaching down through the white billowy vapors. It's a comforting scene, one that reminds me that He's there for me, and ready to help me through every moment of my day. Realistically, I know God's spirit lives within me; closer than my breath (and certainly closer than any cloud), but I'm a visual person, and that image is a warm reminder that He is always there for me.

Looking ahead and visualizing better days is a great exercise. I would often daydream about how much better my life was going to be. I kept telling myself, "Things will be better...soon." I would look into the future at my overall health and relationships and see them as improved. During this time, I also wrote in a journal, and sometimes sketched. I would write my dreams and poetry in a tablet. Basically, I was transferring my thoughts and frustrations on to paper, and it became very helpful. Journaling is not supposed to be difficult or burdensome. It is for our benefit only, and journaling can be as simple or precise as we want it to be. It is something I encourage you to try, for it also can be a good stress reliever.

Who needs a Shrink?

As I mentioned in the body of this book, seeking help from competent professionals is important. I benefited from their services, and I encourage you, your spouse, and your family to give them a try. You will gain insight about your situation, and it will also speed up the healing process. This is not always easy, so be prepared for some difficult sessions, but the time you spend in counseling will certainly help to bring closure to your problem. I firmly believe two heads are better than one when it comes to solving a problem. Your doctor, pastor, rabbi, priest, and especially good friends can help you find a therapist that would be best suited to you. Search until you find someone with whom you feel comfortable. Support groups can also be very good, especially for the short term. Don't hesitate to ask for help. Get involved. It is for your benefit. They are there for you. If money is what stops you, tell them that when you make your first appointment. They often will work with you, or will know how to get additional funding for you. I know a man who bartered for his services.

Reach out of your comfort zone

In our pursuit to find some sort of peace and happiness, it's easy to get caught in a *self-pleasing* mode. We buy things and do things that we hope will make us feel better. We pamper ourselves with nice trinkets and spend money on entertainment, drugs, and alcohol, hoping those activities will alleviate our emotional pain. Those activities certainly help to fill time. However, I found those gratifications to be short lived, and those moments of *highs* soon left me searching for something more enduring.

When I was asked to volunteer as the parish nurse at our church, I learned just how fulfilling volunteering could be. I've done good deeds in the past to feed my own ego, but now I was asked to do it for the benefit of others. I hesitated at first, for after all, I was a busy mom and wife, and was also working, but finally I agreed. Being a parish nurse has taught me a lot. I am convinced that whenever I make a home visit, I am the one who benefits the most. The act of doing for others, as well as the interaction that takes place while volunteering, is a big hug to the heart. Those heartwarming activities help to turn our focus toward the needs of others. They also help to build self-worth. I believe God gives blessings back to those who reach out to others. It's His special treat. It *is* better to give than to receive. Try to do a good deed for another every day. Even a simple task is important.

Places to volunteer are endless. I urge you find an area that interests you and go for it. A great place to start is in your own neighborhood. The elderly love a visit or a batch of cookies any time. Go for a walk, and you will find someone who can use a helping hand or a listening ear. You may choose to be a mentor, a Big Sister or Brother, or volunteer at a school, or for a hospice, read or write letters to shut-ins, play games or cards at care facilities, pass out mail or flowers at the hospital, help with mailings, or volunteer with an animal rescue organization. One friend of mine enjoys volunteering by caring for the flower garden of a shut-in. Even if you can only give a small amount of time, the important thing is to begin, so you can experience the wonderful rewards volunteering brings.

Norman Vincent Peale said in one of his sermons that when we become detached mentally from ourselves, and concentrate on helping people with their difficulties, we are able to cope with our own more effectively.

I'm convinced that those who bring joy into the lives of others can't help but bring it to themselves.

I always end my home visits with a hug. I believe there is power in the human touch. I realize this is not easy for many abuse victims, and many avoid physical contact completely, but that is not healthy. We need to allow people in our lives and allow them to hug us. Not everyone is out to take advantage of us. We should not shut the world out because of our abuse. The more we feel loveable and worthy, the easier hugging becomes. One man told me he hated hugs, but now that he is healthy, he loves them and is the first to offer a hug. Have faith in your intuition, and you will know who—and who not—to hug. Offering a warm hug to a trusted loved one is a good place to start. If touching is very difficult, I recommend getting a pet and start there. Pets are remarkable and can teach us so much. They (usually) are non-threatening and loaded with unconditional love. Animals have a wonderful way of melting the heart and helping us to express love.

Over the years, we have had many pets. Our Diane had a lovebird named Peaches. I was surprised by the amount of love I felt from that tiny bird. It would sit on my shoulder and kiss and snuggle for hours. Who would think a bird could give so much warmth and enjoyment?

Hugging is a natural response, and when we are able to hug, we find we are able to embrace life as well.

Dare to confront

It was extremely difficult to confront my father about the sexual abuse. If my husband hadn't instigated it, it probably wouldn't have happened, at least not for a long time. As I look back, I am so thankful he took charge and made it happen when he did.

Confronting those who injure us is a big deal, and it is an important turn on our journey to health. It helps to retrieve our self-worth, proves our innocence (sometimes), and can prevent the abuse from happening to others. Injury to one's health and spirit is always terribly wrong, and it should never be overlooked or tolerated. By confronting our abuser, we are exercising our right to expose them and make them accountable for their behavior. A counselor is the one to best direct you *when and how* to confront your abuser, so, *follow their advice.* I do know it is important to *never confront your abuser alone.* A loved one, friend, or counselor can certainly assist you when the time comes. Strength and safety comes in numbers. Also, don't attempt to confront your abuser until you are prepared for the consequences. You need to be ready for any response. In some cases, you may need to bring a law officer with you. Before you confront, know what your next course of action will be. Take the advice of your counselor. Again, always have someone with you when you confront—unless, of course, you are writing a letter. Even then, tell someone (and your counselor) what you have done, and make a copy of your letter.

Confronting, however, is not always possible or necessary to one's healing. Each one's situation is different. If you are stuck and feel you should confront, plan to do so. Always pray for wisdom and write out what you want to say prior to confronting. Have clear in your mind the reason you need to confront. You have a right to confront. I wish all who confront their abuser would hear, "I'm sorry. I did you wrong and I feel terrible. Would you please forgive me? What can I do to help you heal? " You deserve to hear those words and I pray you will only, too often, the words are never said.

Some of the responses you can expect from your abuser can be denial, rage, threats, minimizing or justifying the offense, passing the blame, accepting responsibility, and remorse.

Even if your abuser has died, writing them a letter is a good exercise that helps to bring closure. Letter writing is a safe way to vent your frustrations and anger. Don't hold back words. Tell how the abuse has affected your life. I was told to write not only about the reasons I hated my father, but also to state why I loved him. For that, I had to do some searching, but that exercise changed the topic from negative to positive.

While writing, many emotions may surface. You cannot physically vent on your abuser directly, but you can take your anger out on a pillow or punching bag... and really go for it. One person took the toilet plunger and pounded her bed. It is never acceptable or necessary to hurt another or destroy property in order to heal yourself. Crying, yelling, and safely expressing your anger are certainly acceptable behaviors, for a time. This is one time I approve of a private pity party. You are grieving for what was done to you and for the pain you've experienced because of the abuse. But after the party is over, it's time to cross over that bridge and start living the life you were meant to live. And that is a beautiful life.

For me, crying, walking, talking, journaling and sleeping was how I dealt best with my grief and anger. I am not the physical type, so punching wasn't my best choice. I tried punching, but it seemed unnatural and awkward.

Only you know what works best for you; however, you may not know what's best until you've tried it, so be open for suggestions.

And what about the letter? What do you do with it? I recommend you have a private candlelight service, and burn the letter. As the pages disintegrate, that is what we need to do with our haunting past. *Let it go*, and refuse to let the abuse bind you any further. The remaining 28 steps in the beginning of this segment will help you do this.

Plan on confronting your abuser one way or another, and work toward making that happen. It's a very courageous and challenging experience, and one from which you will benefit, one way or another.

After you have confronted your abuser, it's a good time to write a love letter to yourself. In your letter, boast about your strong points, talents, and attributes. Be proud of the person you are, or at least the person you are becoming. Write about your hopes for your future, your dreams, and what you need to do to accomplish them. Set goals and put timelines in your letter. You may want to add inspiring quotes. Now get a picture of yourself and write on the back, "This is a very important person, and I promise to take very good care of this person." Put the picture and letter in an envelope and embrace it. Take this to heart. Besides, you deserve a hug. From time to time, take out the letter and picture. Read the letter again, to see if you are on track. Now look at the picture, and remember how special and loved you are.

Your future is bright and full of opportunities. A new life is waiting ahead of you. I hope I will hear about the new you, and the positive changes you have made in your life. You can write me at *whisperyoursecret@hotmail.com*.

Music, the perfect medicine for the soul

In a music therapy class, I was taught that our bodies respond to relaxing music by producing hormones that lift our spirit, which improves our mood. A relatively new field in health care, *music therapy*, was developed in the 1960s to facilitate this. A wonderful tip that helps in healing is to listen or play uplifting, comforting music. Music truly soothes the soul, so put on your favorite relaxing music as often as you can. It works wonders.

Throughout my book, I have referred to different pieces of music or lyrics that have been meaningful to me. That is because music touches me in a profound way. It was instrumental in my healing; in fact, during my most difficult years, I believe music is what kept me sane. Music was then, and still is, my natural upper.

I love to play the keyboard; however, I never had the patience to study it seriously. I enjoy playing by ear. I would rather create new songs than play what other composers have written. Since I came out with my story, my compositions have held more depth and beauty. Often, I would sit at my keyboard, and within minutes new music would pour out of me effortlessly. Also, inspiring lyrics would come. There were times when I felt so much power in the music that I had to stop playing *and just be still*. During those exceptional moments, I believe I had a miraculous connection with the Almighty.

It says in the "Good Book" that "Every good and perfect gift comes from the Father in Heaven". (James 1:17) I believe that includes the gift of music. God replaced my hours of despair and confusion with beautiful inspiring music. It was His gift to me, and I believe He chose music as a way to reinvent Himself to me, for He knew I wouldn't find Him in the Bible at that time, or from another minister. God spoke *love* to me through my music, and ever since, I have been trying to speak *love* back through it to others. I like to think God plays through my fingers, and that makes me feel special. My music has revived my spirit many times and left me with an incredible peace.

I have since written over 200 compositions and produced twelve CDs. My listeners have told me that my compositions work particularly well, because they are soothing and new, and therefore bring no memories to distract them from receiving the music's benefits. One fan told me my music was anointed - which means to bless. I know it blesses me and I was deeply touched it blessed her, as well. Inscribed on my business cards are the words, *"Music inspired by the hand of God, to touch the hearts of humankind."*

For more great music, you may want to check out Amy Grant's CD "Legacy, Hymns of Faith." It is filled with outstanding music and songs. Also, Giovanni Marradi has many beautiful instrumental albums available. My favorite of his is "Promises". You can find both musicians' music on the Web.

Inspiration for a lifetime

"*Faith*, hope, and love remain but the greatest of these is love." That is what the Bible tells us in I Corinthians 13: 13. I first assumed that having faith in God was the most important thing I could do, but I learned differently in this famous love chapter. It also says that if we have faith to move mountains, but if we have no love, we are just noisemakers, blowing in the wind.

"Love" is indeed an action word. And to help keep us on course, the Bible gives us guidelines to follow so we can be sure we are acting out in love, such as being patient, kind, not boastful or proud or rude, not self-seeking or easily angered; keeping no records of wrong; despising evil, loving truth. It also says love protects, hopes, and perseveres. Those are powerful words to put into action. When we attempt to stay close to God, it becomes easier to love, for His likeness rubs off on us. Our sacrificial acts of love delight God, *for God is in every act of love.* In fact, love is the realm where God works, and when we love, we are automatically elevated to God's workstation. He is there with us in every act of love. I love the example given to me by a friend when I found myself low on love toward another. She suggested I mentally lift one arm up and point it to God, and then point the other arm toward the one I needed to love. In this position I allow God's love to enter me and then flow toward them. I have to admit, at times I run out of love, but God never does. When we fall short on the love end, we only need to ask God for help. He's the filling station for our many needs.

I've learned that my goodness is not measured by the amount of my faith but by the amount of love I bestow. However, my faith is what gave me hope, and that hope softened my heart to where I could forgive my father. The act of forgiving is a gift of love, so "the greatest of these" I believe is indeed *love.*

It bears repeating: Life is challenging enough without us being chained to our past. Regardless of the misfortune, we can't change what happened to us, but we can change our attitude about it. Healing is obtainable. When we allow our misfortune to become a platform for growth, a wiser, more beautiful person emerges. I believe there is a piece of heaven on earth for each of us, if we only dare to find it.

I feel very honored you chose to read my book. If any of what I have said has been beneficial to you, then I am thrilled, for then the purpose of my writing has been fulfilled, and my time and yours has been well spent. Feel free to write or email me and share your story. I'm interested in you. Remember, you don't have to be on this journey alone, but it is up to you to begin. As you do, peace will surely follow. That's a promise.

Jesus said, "I am leaving you with a gift, it is peace of mind and heart. And the peace I give isn't fragile like the peace the world gives. So don't be troubled or afraid." St. John 14: 27.

Peace to you, my friend.

Make your life as great as you are!

Shirley Jo Petersen

Photo by Jim Petersen

The End

Bibliography

A Love Worth Giving, by Max Lucado, W Publishing Group
As A Man Thinketh, by James Allen, self published
Haunted Marriage, by Clark Barshinger, Inter Varsity Press
Holy Bible New International Version Zondervan Bible Publishers
Power Thoughts, by Robert Schuller Harper San Francisco Publishers
Ten Step Cancer Curers, by Lorraine Day M.D.
The Living Bible, Tyndale House Publishers
The Purpose Driven Life, by Rick Warren, Zondervan Publishers
The Power of Positive Thinking, by Norman Vincent Peale, Howel Publications
The Sacred Romance, by Brent Curtis and John Eldredge, Thomas Nelson Publishers
Wounds That Heal, by Stephen Seamands, Inter Varsity Press
whisperyoursecret@hotmail.com author's e-mail
www.SIA.org
www.Raine.org
www.protect.org
www.thelinkup.org (assisting survivors of clergy abuse)
www.openheartsministry.org
www.TroubledWith.com
Michigan Coalition Against Domestic and Sexual Violence
www.mcadsv.org
www.healinprivatewounds.org

Lyrics:
"God Weeps" by Shirley Erena Murray

Recommended Reading

A Safe Place by Jan Morrison

Beauty for Ashes by Joyce Meyer

Breaking the Cycle of Abuse by Beverly Engel

Boundaries by Dr. Henry Cloud and Dr. John Townsend

Captivating by John and Stasi Eldredge

Care of the Soul by Thomas Moore

Changes that Heal by Dr. Henry Cloud

Child Sexual Abuse by Maxine Hancock & Karen Burton Mains

Forgive for Good by Fred Luskin

Grace For The Moment by Max Lucado

Haunted Marriage by Clark Barshinger

Healing for Damaged Emotions by David Deamonds

Holy Humor and Holy Humor Two Cal and Rose Samara

Home Coming by John Bradshaw

How Long Does It Hurt? By Cynthia L. Mather & Kristina E. Debye

If It's Going To Be It's Up To Me by Robert Schuller

My Father's Child by Lynda D. Elliott & Vicki L. Tanner

My Soul's Adventure With Prayers & Turning Hurts Into Halos by Robert Shuller

On the Threshold of Hope by Diane Mandt Langberg, Ph.D.

Reframe your Life by Stephen Arterburn

Secrets of the Heart by Sandra Burdick & Dorie VanStone

Sheet Music – sexual intimacy, Dr. Kevin Leman

Stick A Geranium In Your Hat & Be Happy by Barbara Johnson

The Artists Way by Julia Cameron

The Courage To Heal by Ellen Bass & Laura Davis

The Message Bible, Living Bible, and NIV Bible

The Purpose Driven Life by Rick Warren

The Whisper and Healing Private Wounds manual by Shirley Jo Petersen

The Penny by Joyce Meyer

Why People Don't Heal & How They Can by Caroline Myss

Your Best Life Yet by Joel Osteen

About the Author

Author/Musician/Nurse/Inspirational Speaker

Shirley Jo Petersen is the founder and director of **Healing Private Wounds**, a non-profit faith ministry dedicated to helping victims and families find healing after experiencing the trauma of sexual abuse. Visit www.healingprivatewounds.org

She is an inspirational speaker and leader in promoting sexual abuse awareness and prevention. Shirley is a composer and musician and has produced ten CD's. She participates in a jail ministry for victims of sexual abuse and facilitates two twelve-week sexual abuse recovery groups a year.

Shirley frequently conducts seminars. The topics include; how a victim heals, how to help your loved one heal, how to prevent childhood sexual abuse; how to talk to your child about sexual abuse, spousal sexual abuse and sexual abuse and the law.

Shirley and her husband Jim have four lovely grown daughters, one being a foster daughter.

Her hobbies include traveling, writing, garage sales but most of all being with her family.

Shirley and her husband Jim reside in their lake home in Cadillac Michigan.

You may contact Shirley by phone 231-775-6804 or email her at whisperyoursecret@hotmail.com

Shirley Jo Petersen 1105 Sunset Lane, Cadillac, MI 49601